Stephen,

There is a future for all of us — This thesis will fortify holding the many companies you now own and should give you additional confidence in buying those companies you are considering for your Portfolios.

George

RUST
TO
RICHES

RUST
TO
RICHES

The Coming of the
Second Industrial Revolution

JOHN RUTLEDGE
DEBORAH ALLEN

1817

HARPER & ROW, PUBLISHERS, New York
Grand Rapids, Philadelphia, St. Louis, San Francisco
London, Singapore, Sydney, Tokyo, Toronto

FIRST EDITION

Designed by Alma Orenstein

Library of Congress Cataloging-in-Publication Data

Rutledge, John.
  Rust to riches: the coming of the second industrial revolution/ John Rutledge, Deborah Allen.—1st ed.
    p. cm.
  Includes index.
  ISBN 0-06-015881-6

  1. Industrial management—United States. 2. Portfolio management—United States. 3. United States—Industries. 4. United States—Economic policy—1981– I. Allen, Deborah. II. Title.
HD70.U5R87 1989
338.0973—dc20   88-45905

89 90 91 92 93 AC/RRD 10 9 8 7 6 5 4 3 2 1

To my mom and dad, Isabelle and John Rutledge, who taught me about hard work and taking care of your tools.   —JR

To my family, my constant source of strength.
                                          —DA

Contents

Preface

G ROWING UP in the fifties and sixties when America was the dominant power in the world, and when the words "made in America" meant something to be proud of, we learned from our parents that old-fashioned virtues—"work hard," "save your money," "take care of your tools"—were the keys to lasting prosperity. They were the magic that transformed laborers into craftsmen and turned raw materials into products we could be proud of.

Thirty years later, after working with several governments and hundreds of companies around the world, we still haven't come across any better advice. And these values work just as well for a person or a family as they do for a company or a country. After all, you only need to ask two questions to determine whether a company or a country is going to have a prosperous future: Do the people want to work? Do they have the tools they need to do the job? Hard work and good tools were what made American industry great in the fifties and sixties. Hard work and good tools were the foundation of the German and Japanese growth miracles of the past quarter century and of the recent success stories in Taiwan and Korea. And work and tools will determine how our children are going to live in the next century.

In the eighties it has been fashionable to put down American business. Economists and politicians have been wringing their hands over the budget and trade deficits, telling us that the days when America was a world-class manufacturing power are behind us. They say American workers can't work, that American managers can't manage, and that we face a bleak future with a declining standard of living, a future where everyone will have a job flipping hamburgers, but nobody will be able to earn a decent living. Our lives, they say, will be controlled by our Japanese landlords, who will own our factories, our farms, and the homes we live in.

Our advice to the naysayers is to get back to work. It would be a big mistake to sell American industry short. Equipped with the right tools and incentives, American workers and managers can compete head-to-head with anyone in the world; and our best days are not behind us, they are still ahead. True, American industry went through bad times in the early eighties, but it wasn't bad workers and bad managers that made us unable to compete. It was misguided government policies, which led to bad incentives and worn-out tools. In the late seventies, rising inflation, rising tax rates, and a subsequent proliferation of tax shelters all worked like novocaine to deaden our incentives to work and save and diverted scarce savings dollars into the building of hotels, office buildings, and shopping centers instead of the new machines and factories we needed to compete for world markets.

The reduction of inflation and tax rates and the repeal of most tax shelters in the mid-eighties established a productive new foundation of capital for American industry, and American industry has responded with a vengeance. Tired of getting sand kicked in their face,

American companies have learned valuable lessons from the tough times they endured. They are now "pumping iron"—reducing costs and raising productivity, improving the quality of their products, and relearning the art of managing their scarce capital resources. This renaissance of American manufacturing is producing a second industrial revolution that will make America the preeminent manufacturing power in the nineties.

The key to this turnaround has been getting back to the business of accumulating capital—giving our workers and managers the ability to purchase the tools they need (modern, efficient machines and factories) to produce high-quality products cheaply. In the eighties we began to receive the flood of new machines we needed to jump-start our dying industrial economy—more than $500 billion worth—from abroad through the trade account in a "reverse Marshall Plan." Now machine tools and other capital goods are the fastest growing sectors of our economy at home, too. The modern, efficient U.S. manufacturing companies; the rapidly aging Japanese work force; the capital-hungry developing economies in countries of the Far East, Eastern Europe, and South America; and the political reforms now under way in China and the Soviet Union will combine to create powerful demand for American products, a healthy U.S. trade surplus, and a thriving economy at home in the nineties.

Acknowledgments

T HE IDEAS IN THIS BOOK represent a marriage of economic theory with the practical experience of
working with hundreds of companies as clients of
Claremont Economics Institute over the past fifteen years.
We thank our clients for their many insights and for
sharing their successes and failures with us. We would
especially like to thank Harry Stainbrook, Charles A.
Parker, Michael Tierney, Bruce Johnstone, Herb Gull-
quist, and Dale Frey for the rigorous grillings they gave us
each time we approached them with a new idea.

Thanks also to John Hekman, senior economist at
Claremont Economics Institute, for the important part he
played in developing our ideas and for his moral and
intellectual support during the writing. And thanks to
Kristan Willard for tireless and thorough research in
preparing the illustrations.

We would like to thank Arelo Sederberg and John
Fund for their help and ideas on the structure of the book.

Without the help, cajoling, and encouragement of
Harper & Row, there would have been no book. Thanks to

Harriet Rubin for getting the project started, to Terry Karten for getting it back on track, and to John Michel for turning our efforts into a finished book.

Thanks to our families, who paid the biggest price but get none of the glories.

RUST
TO
RICHES

1

General Who?

A S THOSE OF YOU who survived your first year and still hope to receive your MBAs with the rest of the class of 2041 know," Professor Marshall told his strategic management class, "we don't normally use the case-study method here at the University of Chicago. We prefer to have our students learn the math and the theory first."

After the groans from the students had subsided, Professor Marshall continued. "But next week we are going to make an exception. After two solid months of bending curves and grinding out solutions to equations, we have finally reached the fun part of the course. On Monday we will begin discussing the case of General Motors. The rationale of the case-study method is to learn by identifying and analyzing the mistakes of real managers in actual business situations. That makes GM the perfect case to study, because nowhere in the history of business have so many errors been committed by one well-intentioned group of managers. Destroying the largest and most powerful company in the world was a monumental undertaking for GM's managers, but somehow they managed to pull it off. They made mistakes that were so big, even you people may be able to spot them.

"I'm going to take the last few minutes of class today to give you the flavor of the case. Then, over the weekend, you can study the written case that's being passed around the room, as well as the references listed on the last page of the handout, which are being held for your reading pleasure in the Reserve Room at the library. I especially want everyone to read *Concept of the Corporation,* Peter Drucker's classic analysis of the problems encountered in managing a large organization such as General Motors. And you might also like to read *Call Me Roger,* a very revealing book that details the role played by Roger Smith, GM's final chairman, in accelerating GM's demise. On Monday we'll discuss your study groups' answers to two questions: What caused the downfall of General Motors? And, if you had taken over as GM's CEO in 1981, instead of Roger Smith, what would you have done to turn the company around and steer it into the twenty-first century?"

"General who?" asked Rick Larsen, a student sitting in the back row.

"I'm sorry, Rick," answered Professor Marshall. "I forgot that you have taken a vow not to read your economic history book until the night before the final exam. But maybe it is asking a lot to expect students to know much about a company that went out of business twenty years before they were born. General Motors made cars, lots of them, back in the twentieth century. In fact, for a time between the end of World War II and the late 1980s GM was the largest corporation in the world. General Motors was the country's largest private employer, and accounted, either directly or indirectly through her dealers and suppliers, for more than 2 million jobs. In its heyday, GM had revenues of more than $100 billion per year, manufactured more than 60 percent of all cars sold in America, and was the largest auto maker in the world, bigger than Toyota, Honda, and Hyundai put together."

"If they were so powerful, then why haven't we ever heard of them?" asked Rick. "Why aren't they still making cars?"

"For the same reason the dinosaurs aren't walking down Main Street, Rick. They became extinct. General Motors went out of business more than forty years ago in the early 1990s. GM had so many layers of managerial deadwood that it wasn't able to adapt to a rapidly changing marketplace. They were too big, too slow, and too unresponsive to the changing needs of their customers. When oil prices jumped at the time of the Arab oil embargo in the 1970s, GM was unable to produce the small, fuel-efficient cars their customers wanted, which allowed foreign companies to establish a foothold in the U.S. market. Later, when imports started really eating into GM's market share, GM cried to the federal government for protection, rather than getting down to work to improve their products and lower their costs. But their market share continued to decline all through the 1980s, as you can see from the chart in the handout.

"But it wasn't the imports that killed General Motors. Like all great empires, it died from within. GM's phenomenal growth and rise to power took place under the guiding hand of Alfred Sloan. After decades of dominating the U.S. auto industry under Sloan's leadership, GM's executives began to think they were invincible. But when Sloan stepped down as chairman of the board in 1956, and died in 1966, he left behind a group of successors who were inadequate to the immense task of running General Motors. Without Alfred Sloan to act as a beacon to guide their way, they gradually drifted away from the management principles that had made them successful, and ultimately ran the ship aground.

"GM's early success was the result of a management system forged by Alfred Sloan, an engineer brought in by Pierre du Pont to serve as GM's president and chief executive officer in 1923. Du Pont, as GM's largest shareholder, had been forced to take over the reins as CEO himself when GM's founder, Billy Durant, drove the company into

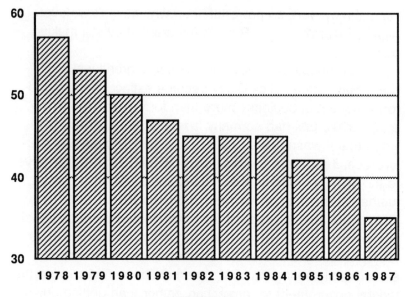

CHART 1.1
GM's U.S. Market Share (%)

the hands of its bankers for the second time in 1920. During Sloan's twenty-six-year tenure as GM's president and CEO, he developed and refined a system of decentralized management that was copied by companies all over the world. In his memoirs, *My Years with General Motors,* Sloan wrote, '. . . good management rests on a reconciliation of centralization and decentralization, or decentralization with coordinated control. Each of the conflicting elements in this concept has its unique results in the operation of a business. From decentralization we get initiative, responsibility, development of personnel, decision close to the facts, flexibility—in short, all the qualities necessary for an organization to adapt to new conditions. From coordination we get efficiencies and economies.'

"Sloan's system had always been embodied in GM's tradition of dividing executive power between a chairman, who was strictly a finance man who controlled the purse strings at the board level, and a strong president, typically an engineer by training, who served as chief executive and ran the operations of the company. Sloan understood the wisdom of letting the engineers build the cars and using the bean counters to handle the money. But it didn't take long after Sloan's departure for his lieutenants to screw it up. Two years after Sloan stepped down as chairman, Frederick Donner staged a palace coup and became the first finance man to be appointed as both chairman and CEO since the days of Pierre du Pont. That was the beginning of the end for General Motors. With power more and more con-centrated in the hands of the chairman and his finance staff, decentralization withered away and GM lost its ability to adapt to change. Needless to say, once the bean counters had stormed the citadel and seized power, they never gave back the keys.

"Then in 1981 the GM board sealed their company's fate by appointing Roger Smith as chairman and CEO. They thought they were hiring a traditional finance guy who would be tough enough to hold down costs and who would be able to manage the assets in GM's sprawling empire. What they got, instead, was a frustrated inventor who, just like Billy Du-rant back in the 1920s, spent money like a drunken sailor. Smith was quoted as saying, 'It's frustrating that we just can't spend the money sometimes as fast as we would like.' In the first half of the 1980s, GM spent $45 billion on new acquisitions and capital equipment. But their break-even level of output went up by 30 percent! Smith once told a press conference back in the 1980s, 'I'm done sweating the details. Now I'm ready to move on to the twenty-first cen-tury.' Well here we are in the twenty-first century. But where is General Motors? Maybe they should have sweated a few more details after all.

"During Smith's tenure as CEO, GM got into lots of businesses where they didn't belong, in the name of tech-nology advancement, and did a really lousy job managing their assets. Ultimately, when their stock price fell below half the book value per share, General Motors was taken over

by an outside group of investors and broken up into separate operating companies. Some were closed down, but
some of them are still operating today . . . under different
ownership, of course. But General Motors itself went down
the smokestack.

"The real irony of the GM story is that GM's slide from
greatness took place during the 1980s, the longest period of
uninterrupted economic growth with low inflation in U.S. history, the period we now refer to as America's second industrial revolution. It was a time when most other American
manufacturing companies were doing things to really get
their acts together. Thousands of companies were restructured by unloading excess assets and refocusing on their
core businesses. There was tremendous growth in plant and
equipment investment, especially in the area of robotics and
automated assembly operations, and manufacturing productivity soared. Ultimately, it may have been the stark contrast
between the good things happening in most American manufacturing companies and the undisciplined spending at GM
that led the wolves to GM's door. I think you'll all enjoy this
case. It has all the ingredients of a good soap opera. On
Monday, I'm sure you'll all be able to tell me the moral of
the story."

Radical Change Is a Fact of Life

It would be hard to find an expert today who would be
willing to consider seriously the idea that General Motors
will be out of business by 1995. In spite of the fact that
they have lost more than ten percentage points of the U.S.
market share in the past five years, and that their stock
has typically been priced by the market at well below the
book value of their assets, GM is just too big a name to
disappear from the American manufacturing scene.

Or is it? Of the twelve companies that made up the
first Dow Jones Industrial Average in 1896, General Elec-

tric is the only company still on the list, a list that included American Cotton Oil, Distilling and Cattle Feeding, Laclede Gas, and Tennessee Coal. And where are Studebaker and Baldwin Locomotive from the 1916 list? Or Postum, Inc., or Nash Motors from the 1928 list? Or Johns-Manville from the 1979 list? Nobody in 1970 would have believed that the Pennsylvania Central Railroad, one of the most powerful companies in the country, could go bankrupt either, or that Texaco and LTV would ever make an appearance in bankruptcy court. History is filled with events a lot more radical than the demise of General Motors.

Economic change is not new. Peter Drucker, in *Innovation and Entrepreneurship*, reminds us that business managers have had to deal with changing business conditions as far back as we have records. And the most successful managers and investors are those who are able to identify, respond to, and exploit change, which Drucker describes as entrepreneurial management.

But it would be difficult to convince the managers and investors who were left shell-shocked after the turbulent changes they experienced in the 1980s that economic change is your friend. After decades of learning how to protect their companies and their portfolios against the ravages of inflation, managers were caught leaning the wrong way when the wind suddenly shifted to deflation, leaving behind enormous casualties in farming, mining, manufacturing, and banking.

The reason why so many people had such a hard time running their businesses in the 1980s was not that they were doing such bad jobs on marketing, production, or managing their people, the traditional skills used to manage the *inside* of a business. It was because they were doing a bad job managing the *outside* of their businesses. They were spending so much time filling out "to do" lists and relating to their workers that they forgot to ask if they were running the right business, with the right capital structure, to fit in with the wholesale changes taking place in the world around them. While they were busy being effective managers, they were sideswiped by economic change.

Business students in the 1970s learned that they should design strategies that protect, or hedge, a company against changes in the economy. Many companies went through all sorts of contortions to hedge their earnings, or their assets, against the danger of inflation by committing their companies to long-term fixed contracts with their suppliers or workers, by borrowing money to finance the purchase of commodities or other key inputs to production, or by distorting their organizational structure with acquisitions of resource-heavy companies that were supposed to do well during periods of high inflation. What they forgot is that it is not as important to have insurance as it is to be insured against the relevant risk.

You may remember the story of the three pigs. The first little pig built his house out of straw. The second little pig built his house out of twigs. And the third little pig, the industrious one, took his time and built a house out of bricks. You see, the third little pig had taken a course in strategic management in business school and understood that it would be worth a certain amount of extra effort to protect his family against the danger of being attacked by the big bad wolf.

In our version of the story, the wolf showed up the next day at the third little pig's house, and, after the appropriate amount of "Little pig, little pig, let me come in" and "No, no, no, not by the hair of my chinny-chin-chin," started huffing and puffing right on cue. Just as he was getting set for a good blow, however, the ground started to shake. Within thirty seconds, an earthquake measuring 8.9 on the Richter scale had leveled the brick house, and both the wolf and the third little pig had been flattened under a pile of falling bricks. And what about the two lazy pigs? Actually, they weren't lazy at all. They had just learned that the San Andreas fault ran directly under their three houses, and knew that the safest structures during an earthquake are those made of flexible materials such as straw and twigs. They divided the third little pig's estate between them and lived happily ever after.

The moral of the story for business managers? As Roseanne Roseannadanna used to say on "Saturday Night Live": "It just goes to show you. It's always something." Businesses face all sorts of risks every day when they open their doors. But it also shows that you can't protect a business against all possible risks. You must choose the one or two that you think are worth paying the costs to protect against. But if you choose the wrong ones, your attempts to protect your business can accelerate your demise.

As our story shows, like it or not, the ultimate success of a business depends as much on whether it is the right kind of business for the world it must operate in as on how well the company is managed. Oil companies, for example, rode the wave of rising oil prices in the 1970s to extraordinary profits. Most of these profits had nothing to do with the quality of a company's management. They were caused by a jump in the price of oil—its product and the principal asset on its books.

Unfortunately, many managers used their windfall to double up their bets—using borrowed money, of course. They figured that if owning a little oil made them rich in the 1970s, then owning a lot more oil would make them a lot richer in the 1980s, proving that Mark Twain was right when he wrote in *Roughing It*, his memoirs from the days of the Silver Rush, "The worst thing that can happen to a man is to win a bet on a horse at an early age."

When oil prices subsequently fell from the mid-thirties to the mid-teens, these companies found themselves in a world of pain. It is interesting to note that the same companies that for years had made a handsome profit when crude oil was selling for two dollars a barrel in the 1950s and 1960s were now losing money with oil prices at fifteen dollars per barrel. It seems that even brief exposure to high oil prices had an irreversible impact on their managers' spending habits. Perhaps that's the behavioral phenomenon that Twain described later in the same book when he wrote about what happened to people when the veins of silver played out and turned to clay. "People easily get reconciled to big money and big prices, and fond and vain of both. It is the descent to little coin and cheap prices that is hardest to bear and slowest to take hold of one's toleration."

Managing Change

A manager who only manages the *inside* of his business is only half a manager. A complete manager will wage war on both fronts by relentless attention to the details of inside management, i.e., by doing a good job of running the operating company, along with continual review of the company's structure to make sure it is positioned to take advantage of opportunities that might be created by changes in the *outside* environment.

By structuring the *inside* of your business, which you can control, to be in harmony with the *outside* of your business, which you cannot control, you can make changes in the business environment work for you. That is the central message in Peter Drucker's *Innovation and Entrepreneurship*. Harnessing change should be viewed as one of the normal objectives in managing a business. In contrast to the popular myth that an entrepreneur is a genius who creates value out of whole cloth, Drucker argues that an entrepreneur is an ordinary person who is trained to systematically *seek out, respond to, and exploit change.*

This book is about managing economic change. We believe there are powerful forces at work today that will make the 1990s just as turbulent as the 1980s, posing enormous risks and providing tremendous opportunities for business managers and investors who know how to manage change. But to exploit the change that will take place in the 1990s, you must first understand it. This book shows how to identify these changes and how to harness their creative power when managing a business or investing money in the 1990s.

Of course, there is no shortage of people who will tell you what will happen in the future. And most of them believe the future looks pretty bleak. Today, it is accepted wisdom among economists, political leaders, and the financial press that the American economy, straining under the burden of the twin budget and trade deficits, and plagued by a chronically low savings rate and the largest foreign debts of any nation in the world, is doomed to being a second-rate industrial power in the 1990s.

We believe they are wrong. While economists and politicians have been wringing their hands over America's allegedly intractable problems, America's business managers have been radically altering the way they run their companies, quietly laying the foundation for a second industrial revolution. We believe this renaissance of American manufacturing will serve as the driving force that will bring a decade of prosperity without inflation and create tremendous investment opportunities for those who understand the process driving the economy.

The reason most economists did such a lousy job forecasting the 1980s, and are likely to miss the boat again in the 1990s, is their single-minded reliance on the country's $4 trillion national income accounts to interpret economic developments. This fixation on current activity levels leads them to ignore pressures developing in our much larger $35 trillion balance sheet that describes our assets, liabilities, and net worth.

Understanding the Two Economies

It is crucial to keep in mind that there are two economies, not one. There is an economy for new goods, services, and new securities, described by the flow of funds and the national income accounts. And there is a separate economy for old goods and old securities. This simple distinction between new and old goods, ignored by traditional macroeconomic theory and practice, turned out to be the secret to understanding the most important economic events of the 1980s, and is the starting point for any serious attempt to see through the fog into the 1990s.

No security analyst would make a judgment about the merits of a company's stock based on the company's profit-and-loss statement alone. He would want to examine its balance sheet as well. Companies don't go broke because they had a bad quarter. They go broke because they run out of capital. To understand the health of a company you must go beyond current sales and profit figures and make a careful analysis of its balance sheet.

The same principle applies when analyzing the economy as a whole. After all, "the economy" is nothing more or less than the collection of all of the people and businesses. Both the current operating characteristics of a country, i.e., its national income accounts, and the condition of its balance sheet must be considered before we can make a guess about its future behavior. This is especially important when you are trying to make sense out of interest rates, stock prices, commodity prices, or currency values. Each are asset prices, not product prices. As such they are more appropriately analyzed from an asset market, or portfolio balance perspective, instead of using the traditional flow-based tools of macroeconomics.

There are two economies, not one—the flow-based *production economy*, described by the national income accounts, and the asset-based *portfolio economy*, described by the balance sheet. The *production economy* deals with the production of new goods and services and with the creation of new securities, i.e., savings and investment. It is the circular flow of income and production explained in chapter 1 of every macroeconomics textbook written since the 1940s. It is measured by the gross national product (GNP), currently nearly $5 trillion for the United States, and is the target of essentially all government efforts to gather and release economic information. When economists talk about "the economy," this is what they mean.

The *portfolio economy* is represented by the country's balance sheet and can be viewed as a fossilized history of all previous economic activity. In it are determined the values of all the old, or existing, goods and securities, and therefore the country's net worth. The portfolio economy does not deal with what we do, but with what we own. And it is enormous. At the end of 1987, there were more than $35 trillion of assets in the United States, more than eight years' total activity in the production economy and nearly twice as much as the gross national product of the entire world.

Under normal conditions the portfolio economy is a sleeping giant. At times when people are just content to own what they already have, the portfolio economy exerts a benign influence over our lives. At such times, we would expect the ordinary tools of macroeconomics to do an adequate job of explaining the direction of the economy. But when abrupt changes in government policies or gaping international differences in asset returns drive a wedge between what people have and what they want, the sleeping giant wakes up. At such times, the synchronous attempts of 240 million people to rebalance the $35 trillion in their portfolios can lead to massive asset price changes that can overwhelm the more ordinary forces at work in the production economy. These are the times of great upheaval, such as the 1970s and the 1980s in the United States, when vast fortunes were made in short periods by people who were able to seize change and use it to their own advantage.

We believe the key to unlocking the secrets of economic change in the 1990s is to focus on the country's capital structure, not on budget deficits, trade deficits, and other flow-of-funds measures of economic activity. As we will describe in later chapters, we believe that the legacy of the 1970s and 1980s is a massive imbalance in the international capital markets. The story of the 1990s will be written in the way the conflicting forces in the capital shortage countries, such as the United States, and the capital surplus countries, such as Japan, are allowed to play out over the next decade.

Chapter 2 points out the true nature of the enormous costs imposed on the United States by the inflationary decade of the 1970s. By the early 1980s, twenty years of high inflation, high tax rates, and tax shelters had diverted our scarce and precious stream of savings dollars away from productive investments and toward stockpiling inflation hedges and tax shelters, leaving us with a legacy of fancy hotels and shining office towers alongside our worn-out factories and tools. If these conditions had been allowed to continue unchecked, the gradual and unavoidable deterioration of American costs and productivity would have made us forever dependent on foreign capital to finance an ever-widening trade deficit. America would have remained a second-rate industrial power forever. But important changes taking place on both sides of the Pacific have begun to alter these trends radically.

Falling inflation and tax reform in the United States in the 1980s produced a prolonged deflation that forced the wholesale write-down of farmland, mining, real estate, and tax shelter assets, and that exposed our chronic shortage of modern, productive industrial capital. This shortage of modern tools and machinery for American industry has set powerful forces in motion that will ultimately reinstate America as a world-class manufacturing power in the 1990s. Historically high real interest rates and intense competition in the marketplace have forced managers to learn how to control costs and improve operating margins. Intense pressure from shareholders to deliver the high returns they have a right to expect in a capital-short economy is making managers use their companies' capital resources more effectively. And all across the Midwest, the part of the country that had become known as the "Rust Bowl," new, efficient factories are being built every day to replace the worn-out relics of the past. Examples of companies that have been totally restructured during the 1980s, and are now reaping the benefits of greater efficiency and leaner balance sheets, include many household names such as General Electric, Goodyear, Bethlehem Steel, and Union Carbide, as well as thousands of smaller companies.

A lot of people have been surprised to see that many of these new factories have foreign names, such as Honda's operations in Marysville, Ohio, or the new Toyota automobile plant in Georgetown, Kentucky. In the same way that American money rebuilt Japan after the war, Japan is now providing a lot of the money that we need to pay for the reindustrialization of America, giving us a jump start to the American retooling process we must go through to regain our former strong position as a world manufacturing power.

Initially, as we describe in chapter 5, many of these tools are being brought into the country from overseas, so they show up as rising imports and a higher trade deficit. But now that these tools are being used to produce low-cost, high-quality products, American companies are finding that they can effectively compete again in world markets. In the mid-1990s, when Japanese investors begin to cash out of their American investments in order to finance an escalating retirement bill at home, American money will replace Japanese money in many of these projects, as our aging Baby Boomers, finally realizing the

importance of saving for their retirement and past the
expensive period of educating their own children, provide
an avalanche of domestic savings to continue our industrial expansion into the twenty-first century.

To be successful in the 1990s, managers must know
how to manage their companies' scarce and expensive
capital resources effectively. As we argue in chapter 7,
they must go beyond traditional concerns about overhead,
operating costs, and profit margins and implement programs for improving the productivity of capital. And they
must be continually on the lookout for opportunities to
prune low-return uses of capital from their businesses,
using as little of their shareholders' capital as possible to
run their businesses.

Our recommendations do not come from abstract
theories—they come from actual boardroom experience.
In the chapters to come, we draw on our experiences working with the managers of more than two hundred companies to lay out the strategies that successful companies
have already used to improve their returns, and that we
believe will be crucial for continued success in the 1990s.

When we look back from the twenty-first century, the
economic change that shook the business landscape in the
1990s will seem terribly obvious. Change is always easier
to understand in the rearview mirror than it is while you
are wrestling with it in the trenches. But judging from the
statements of public officials and the way the economic
news is interpreted by the financial press, this is not at all
obvious today.

We believe that managers and investors who are able
to understand the nature of the changes that will be taking
place in the 1990s will be better equipped to harness the
energy in economic change in running their businesses
and investing their money.

2

The Wrong Stuff

Can America Compete?

NOT SO LONG AGO, the words *Made in Japan* printed on
a product were a warning of shoddy quality. As
H. Ross Perot once said, "I can remember when if
your parents gave you an apple for Christmas you understood, but if they gave you a Japanese toy, you wondered
if they still loved you." That was in the days when the
most exciting Japanese exports were the little umbrellas
that you spear through a maraschino cherry and put in a
whiskey sour. Long before Sony, Toshiba, and Honda
became symbols of high-quality consumer goods. Now,
Made in Japan is the title of a bestselling book by Akio
Morita, chairman and cofounder of Sony, telling the story
of how Japanese companies took on the Goliaths of American industry on their own turf and won. Today, the
American companies who are forced to compete with
Sony, Matsushita, Honda, and Toyota can all agree on one
thing. *Made in Japan* isn't funny anymore.

It doesn't take a rocket scientist to figure out that American manufacturing companies got chewed up by foreign competition in the 1980s. Export markets have shrunk drastically. Importers have captured ever larger shares of the U.S. market. Costs rose while productivity and profit margins fell. Many American companies were forced to make ruthless cutbacks in their operations just to stay alive. By the middle of the decade, more than 1 million workers had been laid off or permanently discharged by American manufacturing companies, and scores of old and inefficient factories had been permanently boarded up. The Midwest industrial states, which ultimately became known as the Rust Bowl, were hit hardest. Rising unemployment in cities such as Chicago, Cleveland, Milwaukee, and Detroit led many people to make comparisons to the Great Depression of the 1930s. In 1985, one of the leading business magazines ran a cover story asking the question that was on everyone's lips, "Can America Compete?"

And there is certainly no shortage of competing theories vying for the honor of explaining the demise of American industry in the first half of the 1980s. Some blame it on the runaway budget deficits, which they say are responsible for both the strong Reagan dollar of the early 1980s and the high interest rates that have been with us for the entire decade. Others say American workers are too lazy or too undisciplined, and not up to the task of competing with highly motivated foreign workers. Or they say that American wages are too high to allow us to compete with the cheap foreign labor available in places such as Japan, Taiwan, Mexico, or Korea. Still others say that the perks and rich life-styles enjoyed by American managers have made them soft, and that they just don't know how to control their costs and run their businesses anymore.

Upon close inspection, most of these arguments don't hold water. Interest rates have declined, as a trend, since

1982, and the dollar has fallen by more than 50 percent since it reached its peak in February 1985, but the trade deficit has remained extremely high by historical standards. Japan, the country with whom we have our biggest trade deficit, is no longer a low-wage country. And somehow, with precisely the same American workers and the same American managers who are now being blamed for our lack of competitiveness throughout the 1980s, we sold enough products to run a modest $3-billion trade surplus in the first year of the decade.

Others take the pessimistic view that the economic events of the 1980s are harbingers of worse things to come. Many observers insist on extrapolating the disturbing trends far into the future. Not surprisingly, they arrive at extremely unpleasant predictions about what's ahead for American industry in the 1990s. They paint images of a powerless, deindustrialized America, the biggest debtor nation in the world, where the cancerous growth of both imports and the service sector have squeezed out all the high-paid manufacturing jobs. In the "McJobs" economy of the 1990s, they say, everybody will have a job flipping burgers at McDonald's, but nobody will be able to earn a decent living.

We believe these dire predictions are nonsense. It doesn't make sense to extrapolate *any* trend overly far into the future. This is especially true with the pseudo-trends of the 1980s, such as high trade deficits, high budget deficits, and low productivity growth, that now comprise accepted wisdom. Extrapolating abnormal conditions far into the future makes interesting cocktail party conversation because the results are always so dramatic. But it's a lousy way to forecast the future. If you conduct the following simple experiment you will see what we mean.

The next time you're in your car on a highway heading west, plot your course for a few miles on a piece of graph paper. Then extrapolate your progress into the future. You will be shocked to find that, even if you begin your journey in New York City, it is only a matter of time before you drive right off the end of the Santa Monica pier. Don't panic at this point. Just pull over to the side of the road and think it over. Chances are the extrapolations are going to be wrong. You will most likely have plenty of time (several days, if you live east of the Mississippi) either to turn left or right or put on your brakes before you get to the coastline. The moral of the story is that blind extrapolation, without a measure of common sense thrown in to tell you what the numbers mean, produces very dramatic but very meaningless results.

The only trends that are legitimate to extrapolate are the ordinary ones, like the sun rising in the east every morning and setting in the west every evening. But nobody ever does that because it's so boring. While extraordinary trends always produce exciting results, they are generally meaningless because *extraordinary trends don't last*. Sooner or later, extraordinary trends always revert to ordinary ones.

And that's why it doesn't make sense to wring our hands about the future of the U.S. economy: The events people are so worried about today—budget deficits, trade deficits, slow productivity growth, and the shrinking manufacturing sector—are not new trends at all. They are the extraordinary and temporary symptoms, i.e., the withdrawal pains, that were created by the extraordinary change in the inflation and tax environment that has taken place over the past decade. As we will describe later in this chapter, inflation and tax rates are the foundation of the economy, just as concrete blocks are used to form the foundation for a house. Ripping out the old foundation and replacing it with a new one, as we have done in the 1980s with falling inflation and tax reform, is a traumatic event.

Fortunately, we don't have to go through multitrillion-dollar restructuring binges every decade. And just like our endless trip west, we shouldn't extrapolate the economic conditions of the 1980s into the future. The key question isn't what would happen to us if we keep restructuring forever. It is what the economy will look like after we have finished rebuilding it; what type of economy will this decade of change leave in its wake? So the purpose of this chapter is to help you to understand what forced these changes to take place and how you can expect them to play out so that you are able to get a handle on the new trends that will emerge in the 1990s.

The key to understanding the problems of American industry in the 1980s is not lazy workers or bad managers. And these problems are not a harbinger of worse things to come. They are simply the price we must now pay for the misguided inflation and tax policies of the 1970s; policies that undermined our base of industrial capital. By offering managers better places to invest corporate cash than plants and equipment, inflation and tax shelters robbed our workers of the tools they needed to produce high-quality products at prices their customers were willing to pay. When you send soldiers to battle armed with slingshots against an enemy driving tanks, you shouldn't blame them for the results. But now, with lower inflation rates, lower tax rates, and fewer ways to shelter income, we are beginning to build capital again. The process of rebuilding our capital base is what this book is all about.

Our Real Problem Is Capital Shortage

The real problem with American industry today is that it is plagued with a massive shortage of productive, usable industrial capital. This capital shortage is limiting its ability to compete in world markets and threatening future improvements in our standard of living. Until our capital deficiency is repaired, we have no more chance of competing with the Japanese in automobiles, machine tools, and electronic equipment than Betsy Ross would have had competing with the operator of a modern sewing machine.

Fortunately for us, however, this is not where the story ends. As we show, the capital shortage itself has set in motion powerful forces that are correcting the problem by changing the incentives for investors and managers alike. These new incentives are forcing our managers to rethink the ways they manage their existing capital assets, leading them to take steps to increase the productivity of capital in their companies. We have begun to use the capital that we have more effectively, and to create new capital goods by building new manufacturing facilities at home and importing equipment from abroad. Given sufficient time, we can repair our damaged capital stock and regain our former position as an industrial power.

Recapitalizing the American economy is a big job; it won't be accomplished overnight. But it is the most important factor driving the American economy today, and it will remain so in the 1990s because more capital will lead to a renaissance of our depressed manufacturing sector, proving all the trend extrapolators wrong. This industrial renaissance will offer tremendous opportunities, allowing the managers and investors who understand the changes taking place to take money and business away from the ones who don't.

The "Wrong Stuff"

A drive across America shows why we have been having such a hard time competing against the Japanese. Twenty years of inflation and tax shelters have diverted our precious flow of savings dollars into producing the "wrong stuff." We have the fanciest hotels in the world with marble lobbies and mahogany-paneled meeting rooms. We have gleaming office towers, with original art on the walls and heated parking garages, to house our corporate headquarters. And we have sprawling shopping centers filled with the latest consumer goods from all corners of the globe. But we still assemble our products in factories built in the 1930s and 1940s. Our machines are worn out and our workers, who are ultimately responsible for getting our products out the door, don't have the tools they need to do their jobs.

In contrast, Japanese hotels are less sumptuous and their executives' offices are modest. In fact, in many Japanese firms the senior executives do not have private offices; they share a room with their colleagues. But their factories are efficient and their workers are armed with the latest in computer and robot technology. They understand that you do not win the battle for international market share in industries like automobiles and electrical machinery with marble hotel lobbies and mirrored office towers. The industrial battle is fought on the factory floor using product quality, reliability, productivity, and price. And its casualties are counted over here in lost jobs, shrinking market share, and boarded-up factories. Hotels, office buildings, and shopping centers consume our wealth. Factories, machines, and tools produce it.

A typical manufacturing worker in Japan, according to recent World Bank estimates, has almost twice as much capital to work with as does his counterpart in American manufacturing, as shown in chart 2.1 on page 24. This— not cheap foreign labor—explains why the battle hasn't been going our way so far.

In the past decade, rising costs, falling productivity, and a growing reputation for poor product quality have turned the United States into a second-rate industrial power. For example, in 1968, imports made up only 7.3 percent of the U.S. auto market. In 1979 they broke the 20 percent barrier for the first time. Today they account for 31 percent of all cars sold in America and are still growing. And it wasn't all done with low import prices and cheap foreign labor. Recent surveys by J. D. Powers and Associ-

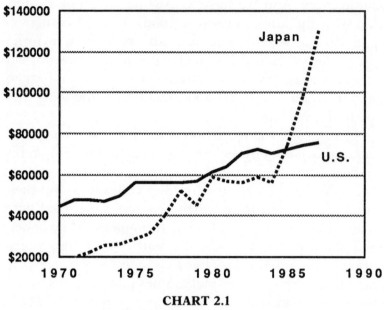

CHART 2.1
Capital per Worker: U.S. and Japan

ates show that of the ten makes of car whose owners were most satisfied with their purchase after one year of ownership, eight are foreign, and of the eight, six are Japanese. The story is the same in color televisions, video cassette recorders, cameras, and lap-top computers.

In some cases, we are getting just what we deserve. General Motors' senior management, for example, played an active role in building their own coffin. General Motors once dominated the automobile industry with 52 percent of the domestic market. But between 1978 and 1987, as we describe in chapter 7, GM's share of the U.S. market fell by more than 16 percentage points, from 52 percent to 36 percent; that's a 31 percent erosion in their unit volume in only nine years, enough to account for more than $100 billion, or one-third of the total U.S. net foreign debt position at the end of 1987! During the 1980s, GM spent more than $50 billion to prove that chairman Roger Smith's grand vision of the "corporation of the twenty-first century" was actually a hallucination. So at the end of the day when the beans had all been counted, General Motors' break-even level went up. In other words, they had to produce more cars just to cover their overhead than they did before Smith took over, *and* their profits went down.

The General Motors story, however, is the exception, not the rule. Most companies are managed by competent and hard-working managers who do their best to make profits. Our real problem is not that our workers can't work or our managers can't manage, but that neither have the capital equipment they need, where they need it, to do the job. We simply don't have the tools we need to produce the high-quality, low-cost products that our consumers have a right to expect for their money. For the past twenty years, while our flirtation with inflation and tax shelters has been bleeding off our savings into making the wrong stuff, Japan, Taiwan, Korea, and other countries have pressed steadily forward with massive capital accumulation efforts, building an armada of industrial plants and equipment. This puts American workers at an extreme competitive disadvantage in the world marketplace. It's very romantic to read stories of David, armed only with a stone and a slingshot, doing battle with the armored, sword-bearing Goliath. But it's a dumb way to go to war. David only beats Goliath in the storybooks. In the real world Goliath wins every time.

What Is Capital?

Capital is a word that has many different meanings— money in your pocket, the net worth of a business, an expression of approval, the seat of a government. We will use the term *capital* to mean *capital goods*—the tools, plants, and equipment we use to produce more output. Capital is the stuff that allows us to get more product from a day of labor and other resources than we could get with our bare hands alone. A skilled carpenter, for example, can frame a house a lot faster with a claw hammer and a Skilsaw than he could with a heavy rock and a sharp stick. A farmer can grow more grain with a tractor, a planter, a cultivator, and a harvester than he could with his hands alone. And a seamstress can sew more dresses with a sewing machine than with a needle and thread.

By the term *capital stock* we mean the accumulated stockpile of all our existing capital goods—all the hammers, tractors, and sewing machines—measured at a given date. Capital has to do with our accumulated assets, not with economic activity: It refers to what we *have*, not what we *do*. It represents all the goods that we have produced in the past but have not yet used up, the goods that we have been patient enough to withhold from consumption in the hope of raising our future standard of living—a sort of productive savings account. Capital stock plays the same role for an industrial economy as does the seed corn that the farmer puts aside from this year's crop in order to plant a new crop next spring. As such, it represents the primary link between the past, the present, and the future in economic analysis.

For more than two hundred years, economists have known that capital accumulation is a necessary condition for continued economic advancement. As long ago as 1776, in *An Inquiry into the Nature and Causes of the Wealth of Nations*, Adam Smith wrote:

> Wherever capital predominates, industry
> prevails. . . . Every increase or diminution of capital,
> therefore, naturally tends to increase or diminish
> the real quantity of industry, the number of produc-
> tive hands, and consequently the exchangeable
> value of the annual produce of the land and labour
> of the country, the real wealth and revenue of its
> inhabitants.

Or, later in the same book:

> When we compare, therefore, the state of a nation
> at two different periods, and find that the annual
> produce of its land and labour are evidently greater
> at the latter than at the former, that its lands are
> better cultivated, its manufactures more numerous
> and more flourishing, and its trade more extensive,
> we may be assured that its capital must have in-
> creased during the interval between those two
> periods. . . .

John Stuart Mill, another of the fathers of classical economics,* wrote in 1848 in *Principles of Political Economy:* "The productive industry of every country is in proportion to its capital; increases when its capital increases; and declines when it declines." And he showed an appreciation for the fact that the living standard of the typical worker rises and falls with the amount of capital at his disposal:

> Universally, then, we may affirm, that, other things
> remaining the same, if the ratio which capital and
> population bear to one another remains the same,
> wages will remain the same; if the ratio which capi-
> tal bears to population increases, wages will rise; if
> the ratio which population bears to capital
> increases, wages will fall.

In fact, virtually every important treatise on political economy written before the Great Depression devoted major sections of their analyses to the factors influencing capital accumulation. None of them would have been surprised to learn that a country that had allowed itself to fall behind in saving and accumulating capital goods

---

* Later in the same section Mill states, "There is land, such as the sands of Arabia, which yields nothing." Even great men do not have perfect foresight.

would lose its preeminent position in the world economy. Unfortunately, the Great Depression changed the focus among economists from political economy—the study of how nations create wealth—to macroeconomics—the study of how governments can influence a society's current income— and switched the emphasis in economic analysis from long-term capital accumulation to unemployment rates. As it turned out, we could have used an Adam Smith or a John Stuart Mill in the 1970s to blow the whistle on the long-term damage that rapid inflation and bountiful tax shelters were doing to our capital stock.

We should also be careful to distinguish the difference between "capital formation" and saving. A society has two ways to transfer today's work into tomorrow's consumption. It can make consumer goods now, store them up, and consume them in the future, roughly the equivalent of canning tomatoes in the summer to eat during the winter. Or it can build tools today that will make its workers more *productive* in the future, such as computer-operated assembly lines to produce more cars for less money sometime down the road. Both represent saving, but only the latter creates capital goods. Stored up consumption goods do allow you to consume today's work in the future; but unfortunately you can only consume them once, then they are gone. Capital goods, however, can be used to produce consumer goods again and again in the future—they have more kick in producing future living standards.

Our stockpiles of grains, our houses, our automobiles, and our refrigerators and other durable goods, which amounted to more than $1 trillion at the end of 1987, represent a very important way that we have been able to save for the future and transfer today's sweat into tomorrow's consumption. They would continue to provide us with services in the future, even if no economic activity at all were simultaneously taking place.

From this we can also see that while all saving does not create capital goods, all creation of capital goods does require saving. A society that consumes all of its output every year can never accumulate capital, hence will not enjoy a rising standard of living. As we will see in chapters 3 and 4, the large gap between savings rates in the United States and savings rates in the fast-growing countries of the Far East has been the third important factor, along with inflation and taxes (and inflation and high tax rates have been partially to blame for the decreased savings rate), in creating the capital shortage we face today.

The easiest way to understand the importance of capital goods in determining our living standard is to imagine life without them. Imagine if you were to exchange places with a person living in Ethiopia where they have neither our resources nor our capital stock. How long would it take before your children were hungry and Ethiopian children were applying to Stanford Business School? It may seem obvious, but it is an important point that it is not our wit and wisdom alone that have made us so rich, but the immense stockpile of capital goods we inherited from our predecessors.

In a world of no capital goods there would be no computers, no copy machines, no tractors, no airplanes, and no sewing machines. Since we can only consume what we produce, the vastly reduced amount of work that we would each be able to accomplish without capital goods would drastically reduce the total output of the economy. We would quickly revert to the standard of living of primitive man. Indeed, that is precisely the position of the poorest countries in the world today, the ones where there is the least capital per worker. As the histories of Western Europe, America, Japan, and now Korea show, accumulating capital goods is at least a necessary ingredient to becoming a great industrial power.

As a general rule, the greater the amount of capital goods per worker in a given country, the higher will be the productivity of each worker and his standard of living, as shown in chart 2.2 on page 30. Most estimates suggest that

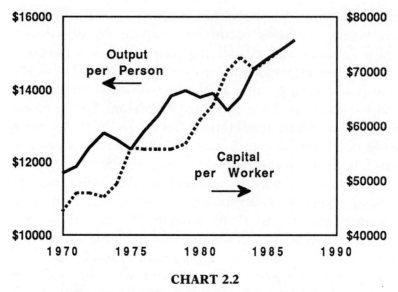

CHART 2.2
More Capital Means Higher Living Standards

increasing the stock of capital by 1 percent, with labor unchanged, will raise output by about 0.3 percent; increasing the amount of labor by 1 percent will increase output by about 0.7 percent; and increasing both capital and labor together by 1 percent (which leaves their relative proportions unchanged) will increase total output by 1 percent. In addition, these estimates generally allow for the historical fact that there is a tendency for the same mix of inputs to produce a little more output each year than the previous year, due to improvements in technology and knowledge.

Today in the United States, even after the damage our capital base has suffered in the past decade, we have the largest stock of capital goods ever assembled on the face of the earth. As chart 2.3 shows, at the end of 1987 our stock of capital goods was valued at approximately $4.1 trillion, composed of about half capital equipment ($2.0 trillion) and half structures ($2.1 trillion). In 1987, using those capital goods, we were able to produce $4.5 trillion worth of goods and services. In per worker terms, however, we

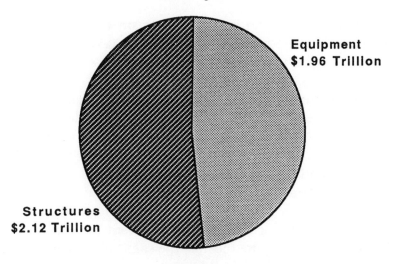

**Equipment
$1.96 Trillion**

**Structures
$2.12 Trillion**

CHART 2.3
U.S. Capital Stock: 1987

were passed by Japan in 1985, where manufacturing workers now have about 70 percent more capital per worker than American workers. It is this per worker difference that shows up so clearly in loss of competitiveness.

How Did We Get the Wrong Stuff?

Our current stockpile of tangible goods, including all the hotels, office buildings, and shopping centers as well as the factories and equipment, didn't just drop out of the sky one clear night. It was built up over many years, like an immense wine cellar. Each year we add part of that year's harvest of new assets to our stockpile and take out what we used up or what went bad during the course of the previous year. And, like the wine cellar, the stock of real assets has vintages. You can read them on the cornerstone of the hotel or the factory, the serial number visible through the window of the automobile, or the model number of the stamping press. This reminds us that the creation of each capital asset was once the conscious decision of some investor or group of investors, *based on all of the information available at the time the decision was made.*

Unfortunately, as we shall see below, when investors receive systematically bad information over a long period of time, they make systematically bad investment decisions. And once those bad decisions have become fossilized in bricks and mortar, they are not recallable.

Capital information is a little like the children's game of Lincoln Logs, where you use the same logs, doors, and windows to produce all sorts of different buildings. The same bricks, the same mortar, the same steel beams, and the same hard-hat labor that were used to build a resort hotel in Tampa in the 1970s could have been used to build a modern, efficient auto parts factory in Buffalo.

But that's where the comparison ends. Lincoln Logs are reusable—hotels are forever. Unlike Lincoln Logs, where you can take the log cabin apart after you have made it and build a barn out of the pieces, creating capital goods is a one-way street. Once a new hotel has been built, it can't be taken apart and turned into an auto parts factory.

For example, assume that an investor, after comparing the after-tax returns he could expect from building a new hotel or building a new factory, decides it is more profitable to build the hotel. Later, after the hotel has been built and opened for business, the government announces a new tax to be paid by all hotel owners, equal to 10 percent of annual revenues. If the owner had known about the tax before building the hotel, he would certainly have altered his calculations about the relative attractiveness of hotels and factories. The new information could even have tipped the scales and convinced him to build the factory instead of the hotel. Once he has already built the hotel, however, such calculations are academic—these aren't Lincoln Logs and it's too late to change his mind.

Once a capital good has been built, new information about its returns can affect its price, but not its existence. In our example we would expect the hotel tax to push the price of all of the existing hotels down, by lowering their returns and making them less attractive to own. This drop in the returns and resale value of hotels, of course, would convince future investors to build fewer hotels, or even none at all. And it would raise further questions about the economy. How much would the falling hotel prices reduce the net worth of the hotel owners? Would they remain solvent? Would their spending patterns change? What about the impact of falling hotel prices on the banks that hold the deeds to the hotels as collateral against the loans they made to build them? Would they go out of business?

But whatever happens, an investor would not be able to turn the hotel into a car factory simply because he has new information. Like a fly trapped in amber, the investor's information about the relative returns of alternative investments is frozen at the point the structure is built. But the resulting capital good will be with us for a long time. In that sense, today's capital stock represents a fossilized history of the information available to investors at various points in the past.

The decision to build a hotel, as opposed to a new factory, of course, is made by individual investors based on the costs, revenues, and after-tax rates of return they expect over the useful life of the project. Therefore, our argument that something has systematically skewed our asset base toward too many shopping centers and not enough factories implies that something must have changed the information used by investors to compare the relative attractiveness of alternative investments during the years we were building up our current wine cellar of assets. Otherwise, investors would not have made the decisions in the way they did.

That something, of course, was government policy. The steady rise of inflation and tax rates from the middle of the 1960s to the end of the 1970s, together with the proliferation of tax shelters designed to allow investors to avoid paying taxes on certain categories of assets, had profound effects on the desirability of different types of assets. In many cases, such policy effects overwhelmed the normal economic considerations, and unproductive capital assets were built strictly as inflation hedges or tax shelters. This had devastating effects on the economy, not in terms of what we did, but in terms of what we didn't do with the resources we used to build inflation hedges and tax shelters. Inflation and tax policies during the 1970s systematically deflected the energies of American savers and investors into building the wrong capital assets. Based on distorted information, they built temples for worshipping consumption, rather than tools to produce products. And just as it took a long time to create the problem, it is going to take a long time to work our way out of it. We can only rebuild our stock of industrial capital one factory and one machine at a time.

How We Got Hooked on Inflation and Tax Shelters

Economists have known for a long time that inflation and tax policy have important effects on the economy. But, for the most part, they typically restrict their analyses to the ways in which inflation and taxes affect *current* economic activity. They look at the ways changes in inflation and tax rates alter the distribution of income (like the fact that inflation lowers the living standards of pensioners and other people on fixed incomes), the ways they affect incentives for working and saving, and how they affect the way people spend their money.

These effects are important, but changing inflation and tax conditions assert their most powerful effects on the economy in a much different way. By altering the delicate balance between the rates of return on different assets, inflation and tax policy influence people's asset demands—the way they choose to divide up their wealth among different types of investments. Radical changes in investment preferences play havoc with the prices of existing assets, which, in turn, affect people's net worth, economic activity, the solvency of the entire financial system, and the capital stock itself. This has been especially true in the 1980s. Bank failures, Latin American loans, the farming crisis, real estate problems, and the demise of the oil patch and the Texas Savings and Loans were all caused by falling asset prices, not by lack of income. It is the asset markets, not the income flows, that explain the major events of the 1980s.

The way in which investors choose to hold their wealth, of course, is entirely up to them. If they want to, they can keep it all in the bank. They can put it in the stock market. Or they can stuff it in their mattresses. Most investors, however, don't like to keep all of their eggs in any one basket. They keep a portion of their money in the bank; some as equity in their home; some in stocks, bonds, or mutual funds; some in real estate investments; and perhaps some in gold coins, stamp collections, or used cars. By diversifying their holdings across many different types of assets, investors hope to accomplish several different objectives at once—liquidity, safety, rate of return—while reducing their exposure to anything that might go wrong in any one area.

Common sense would tell us that investors decide how much of their net worth to keep in each type of investment—how to slice up their net worth pie—based on each asset's relative risks and returns. If investors expect stock market investments to yield a return 20 percent higher than real estate investments, for example, we would expect investors to devote a larger slice of their net worth pie to stocks and a smaller one to real estate than they would in a situation where they expect the returns to be the same. Or, if they are extremely optimistic about gold prices, they will hold a larger slice of the pie in gold and, therefore, a smaller slice in all other investments, and so on. This idea of *portfolio balance*, that investors balance their holdings of different assets based on their relative returns and risks, is at the heart of how we got ourselves into the capital-short spot we're in today.

In practice, the most simple, and perhaps the most important, decision that investors make is the way they split their wealth between hard or *tangible assets*, such as houses, cars, boats, and gold coins, and paper or *financial assets*, such as stocks, bonds, and bank accounts. That's because the values of these two types of investments are affected so differently by changes in economic conditions. Returns made by investors on tangible assets tend to be *service flows, price appreciation*, and *tax benefits*—items that are strongly affected by changes in inflation and tax rates. Returns on financial assets, however, tend to be paid in cold, hard cash, and are very sensitive instead to changes in interest rates.

For example, most people don't think of their house as an asset, with a rate of return, even though it is the largest single investment they are likely ever to make. The return on owning your home is partly a service flow—the amount of rent you would otherwise have to pay each month if you didn't own the house, the enjoyment you get from your freedom to pound nails in the walls any time you want, the joy of participating in the "great American dream," and so forth. This service flow is non-taxable, because it cannot be measured and recorded on your income tax statement.

Another component of the return on your house is the appreciation you expect in the price each year, over and above the costs of maintaining the property. (Homeowners in Houston and Tulsa were surprised to learn, during the oil bust of the 1980s, that this portion can be less than zero.) And part of the return is the fact that you can deduct the interest portion of your mortgage payment from your taxable income when figuring your tax bill. Add them all together and you have at least a guess at the rate of return on your house when it is viewed as an investment.

In comparison, the rate of return on most financial assets is much simpler to figure. If Treasury bill rates are 6 percent, you get a 6 percent return by owning a Treasury bill. Likewise, the return on a bond is the sum of the interest payments and any capital price appreciation or depreciation expected during the year, and the return on a stock is the sum of the dividends and any expected price appreciation or depreciation. With the exception of the interest from municipal bonds, the returns from financial assets are generally taxable, so most financial assets don't serve as useful tax shelters. And, historically, the prices of financial assets don't go up with the general price level, so inflation is not your friend either. Ultimately, it is comparisons of the returns between the tangible assets and the financial assets after taxes— colored by the investor's perceptions of the riskiness and liquidity of each—that the investor uses to determine what proportion of his or her portfolio to hold in each category.

At the end of 1987, American investors had their wealth divided between tangible and financial assets in the proportions shown in chart 2.4 on page 38. As you can see, of the $36.4 trillion of assets owned by investors at the end of 1987, $14.2 trillion, or 39 percent, were held in the form of tangible assets, such as hotels and shopping centers, and $22.2 trillion, or 61 percent, were held in the form of financial assets, such as stocks and bonds and savings deposits. These represent aggregate numbers for the economy, not for an individual investor, of course, but they also can be viewed as the asset demand, or desired asset mix, of a hypothetical "average investor." Since each investor is free to divide his portfolio between tangible and financial assets in any way he wishes—i.e., no investor is forced to hold a given mix of assets—the observed mix at any time must represent the mix demanded by investors based on the assets' relative returns.

The best way to see this is to imagine that it were not true. What would happen if investors' actual assets were different from their desired assets, if actual assets were divided in the way shown in chart 2.4, but investors wanted their assets split precisely half in tangibles and half in financial assets? In that case, investors would demand more tangible assets than currently exist—$4 trillion more to be precise—and there would be a matching $4 trillion surplus of financial assets. It follows that each investor would try to sell some of his stocks or bonds in order to increase his holdings of tangible assets. But there would be no investors willing to take the other side of the deal. No investor would want to buy the unwanted stocks and bonds, and no investor would be willing to sell the tangible assets that investors want to buy, at least not at the existing prices. Like the game of musical chairs where the music stops and someone is left standing without a chair, this could not work. Something would have to give.

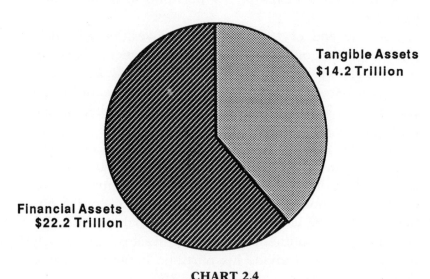

**Tangible Assets
$14.2 Trillion**

**Financial Assets
$22.2 Trillion**

CHART 2.4
Total U.S. Assets: 1987

What gives, of course, are prices. Eager hard asset buyers would soon push hard asset prices higher and eager paper asset sellers would push security prices lower. At the end of the day, when the dealing is over, a kind of financial magic will have taken place. Valued at their new prices—higher prices for hard assets and lower prices for securities—hard assets would have become a larger share and securities would have become a smaller share of investors' portfolios. These price adjustments would continue until a state is reached where investors are content to hold the existing stocks of assets. That's the point where the music can stop with everyone able to sit down again.

This is the key to understanding the concept of portfolio balance. Asset demands can change at a moment's notice. But at any given moment the physical stock of assets is fixed. Since assets must be owned by someone in a more or less voluntary way all of the time, this means that asset prices will move in whatever direction necessary to make investors willing to hold the existing stock of assets.

Now, because the demands of investors for various assets depend on their views about the relative returns on each asset, any policies that alter the attractiveness of owning a particular asset will show up as sudden changes in asset prices. And changing asset prices, relative to the cost of producing new office buildings, shopping centers, factories, and hotels, will have dramatic effects on which ones investors decide to produce and add to our capital stock. A 10 percent tax abatement on hotels, for example, would quickly make investors bid up the price of hotels to a higher level reflecting the value of the tax savings. Higher hotel prices, in turn, would make real estate developers flock to hotel construction, and would make their bankers willing to loan them the money. And that is how events in the 1970s led us to produce a boatload of the wrong stuff.

The 1970s represented a high-water mark in destructive policymaking, having created the most massive and disruptive policy distortion to the economy's asset markets that we have experienced since the Great Depression. The single largest source of damage was inflation, which effectively subsidized the ownership of tangible assets at the expense of securities and made investors turn their portfolios inside out. For example, if the general price level, and therefore the price of goods, including houses, is rising at 10 percent per year, then the owner of a $100,000 house is receiving a $10,000 subsidy per year, in the form of a higher resale value and increasing equity in the house. In the language above, 10 percent inflation tilts the investor's asset demand decision in favor of more tangible assets and fewer financial assets.

This increase in net worth—basically, being paid for watching the value of your house go up—is extremely destructive for the economy. It undermines incentives for working, since it is much easier to earn by watching than earn by sweating, and it undermines incentives for saving. People save in order to increase their net worth, so they can use the money later in life during illness or retirement. But if rising housing prices are increasing your net worth, then why dip into your paycheck to feed your savings account? As it turned out, these increases in net worth tended to make people spend *more* money, not less, which they financed by borrowing. As we will see in chapter 3, this compounded the already lousy savings habits of the Baby Boom generation and worsened America's severe savings shortfall during the past decade.

Worse yet, paying a subsidy to people for owning a house soon changes their investment decisions. It's only human. If you paid $5 every day for a week to each child who rode a red bike to school, you can be sure that by the following Monday, you'd see a lot more red bikes in the bike rack—after all, red spray paint is only $2 a can. It's the same with inflation. Chart 2.5, comparing the total cumulative return on owning tangible assets, such as oil

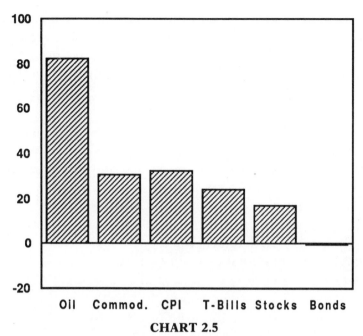

CHART 2.5
Asset Returns: 1977–1979 (%)

and commodities, with different financial assets, shows the facts that were staring investors in the face in the late 1970s. Due to the inflation subsidy for owning hard assets, their returns far exceeded those available on securities, and compared to such terrific advantages, the return on long-term Treasury bonds looked unimpressive. Since the only way to collect the inflation subsidy was to own a house, or some other inflation hedge, and since the bigger the house, the bigger the subsidy that you collected, inflation made people want to own more and bigger houses than they would have wanted to own if prices were stable.

So people began to do things to contort their personal and business portfolios of assets so as to collect as much of the money the government was handing out as possible. Before long, people were buying houses they didn't need, but swore they did. And businesses were borrowing money to buy more farmland, fancy office buildings, works of art, and subsidiaries in the commodity business. In each case, they justified their investments as prudent protection against the danger of further inflation. But by the time they were finished, they hadn't just protected themselves against inflation, they needed it to stay afloat.

Changes in the tax code during the 1970s had the same effect. Since part of the return on owning tangible assets is both unmeasured and untaxed—e.g., the service flow value of owning your house—increasing tax rates, like the ones we experienced in the 1970s, fell more heavily on the income from securities than they did on tangible assets. Therefore, higher tax rates made people shift their asset demands from stocks, bonds, and money market accounts to real estate and other tangible assets. In addition, the proliferation of tax shelters in the 1970s, which often required the investor to own an oil rig, an apartment building, or some other tangible asset to get a tax break, had the same effect. Taken together, the triple subsidy of inflation, high tax rates, and tax shelters proved to be a package the investors couldn't ignore. They abandoned the securities markets en masse to seek refuge in inflation hedges and tax shelters. And they spent more and more of their energies devising new ways to milk money out of the government and profit from rising prices, and less and less on finding ways to produce the products their customers wanted at prices they were willing to pay.

You can see how rising inflation and tax shelters changed investors' behavior in chart 2.6. In 1972 people held only 39 percent of their wealth as tangible assets and the remaining 61 percent in financial assets. Because of the inflation, rising tax rates, and increased tax shelters during the 1970s, however, investors steadily increased their tangible asset holdings to 45 percent of their portfolios by 1980. That 6 percent increase may not sound like much as a percentage, but remember that we are talking about an enormous total portfolio, which was valued in

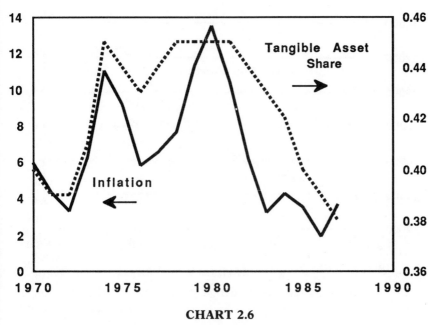

CHART 2.6

Inflation and the Tangible Asset Share (%)

1980 at more than $21 trillion. So the shift in asset demands caused by inflation and tax policy increased the demand to hold our fixed stock of hard assets by more than $1.3 trillion. Since the only other asset investors can hold is financial assets, this entire $1.3 trillion increase in desired tangible-asset holdings was matched by an equal reduction in investor demand to hold securities. As we discussed above, sudden shifts in asset demands of this sort exert *all* of their initial impact on asset *prices*. It takes time to build new ones and wear out old ones. Not surprisingly, the shifts in asset demands shown in chart 2.6 created roaring bull markets in commodities, farmland, oil, metals, and real estate, and led to a decade of bear markets in both stocks and bonds.

The skyrocketing commodity prices turned a lot of innocent bystanders into overnight millionaires and led to phenomenal net worth increases for the country as a whole, as shown in chart 2.7. Chart 2.7 on page 44 shows

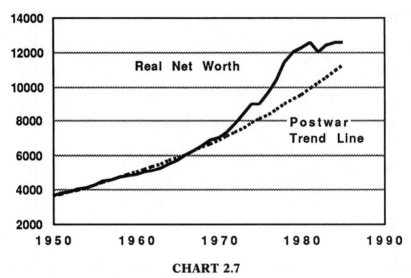

CHART 2.7
The 1970s Net Worth Bulge (in billions of 1985 $)

the bulge in actual net worth, relative to our postwar trend, that occurred in the late 1970s. This bulge, reproduced in chart 2.8, reached a peak in 1980, by which time U.S. net worth had increased by more than $2.5 trillion compared with its postwar trend. That's real money, even to a politician.

Of course all that net worth just got us into more trouble, as illustrated by what happened to the farmers. Like the miners during the Silver Rush that Mark Twain wrote about in *Roughing It*, farmers would have been more or less than human if they hadn't gone crazy, just as the rest of us did, in the presence of all that net worth. Good farmland in Minnesota, for example, increased in price from about $1,000 per acre in 1970 to $4,000 per acre in 1980. Like a balloon filling with hot air, the net worth of a farmer who happened to own 1,000 acres of the stuff increased by $3 million. But he was the poorest rich man in town. The land wasn't any better, so it wouldn't grow more corn than before, and he didn't have any more money to spend than before. The only thing the farmer

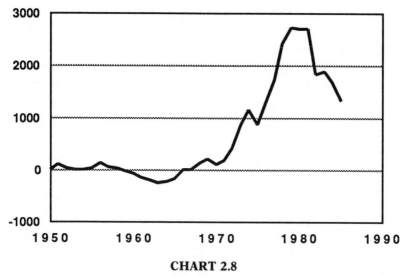

CHART 2.8

Excess Net Worth (in billions of 1985 $)

could do was sit on his front porch in a rocking chair and look at his wealth. He couldn't take his wife to dinner, he couldn't afford to take a vacation, and he didn't have the money to send his children to college, at least not without selling the land. But he didn't want to do that. Farmland was too great an investment!

But one day a big limousine pulled up in the drive-way, and a banker stepped out. "Mr. Farmer," said the banker, "I can solve your problem. You have a lot of net worth but no money. I have lots of money, and I'd like to loan it to you. All we have to do is use your appreciating farmland as collateral for the loans. That way you can do all the things you want and still keep the land. Besides, the way things are going, you won't have any trouble paying off the money you'll owe me—you can pay it out of the increased value of the land after you have retired." So the farmer and the banker had a deal. Neither knew at the time that they were simply wrapping papier-mâché debts around a balloon of net worth; or that there was nothing in the balloon but hot air.

But by far, the most damaging effects of inflation and tax shelters were on our stock of capital. Inflation and tax shelters, by distorting asset prices, also distorted the types of new capital goods we produced. By pushing up the prices of hotels, office buildings, and other inflation hedges and tax shelter assets, these destructive policies created overwhelming incentives for people to build more of them. So we began adding to our stockpiles of oil rigs and office buildings at an unprecedented rate, using the same resources we would otherwise have committed to new factories and machines. For example, between 1970 and 1980, the stock of existing oil rigs more than tripled and the supply of office space more than doubled, due to the high prices and high profit margins their builders could collect.

Meanwhile, because the bond and stock markets—the sources of corporate funding—were rapidly shrinking the money available to companies to expand, their industrial capital had all but dried up. Every dollar of new capital investment undertaken by corporate managers must come from the securities markets, through stock or bond issues or through retained profits. But with interest rates up and security prices down, managers decided it was too expensive to build; instead of issuing stocks and bonds to raise money for new plants they would make do with old capital instead. The result was that over a number of years in the 1970s, as our aging factories and capital equipment wore out, we replaced them not with new factories and new capital equipment but with hotels and office buildings (items that enjoyed tax advantages). And once the new stock of inflation hedges and tax shelters had been put in place, we began to *need* inflation and tax shelters to justify their returns. We had learned to live with inflation and tax shelters so well that we were hooked on them, as an addict is hooked on drugs. We felt rich, and we lived like kings. In all probability we could have continued to do so for a while longer, mindless of the damage we had done by eating our seed corn, if high inflation and tax shelters had remained in place. But all the while we had been building the wrong stuff for competing effectively in world markets for manufactured goods.

Withdrawal Pains

In the 1980s, the bill for these disastrous policies came due. Falling inflation and tax reform put us through a cold-turkey withdrawal from our inflation and tax habit. Soon after President Reagan took office in 1981, the inflation rate headed south. From a peak of 14 percent in 1980, the rate of consumer price inflation tumbled to only 1.6 percent in 1986. And President Reagan's tax reform campaign brought the top marginal tax rate on income from 70 percent the day he took office to only 28 percent in 1989, and most of the tax shelters were stripped from the tax code. Investors, after more than a decade of diligently preparing for inflation and tax shelters, were caught totally by surprise, all dressed up for a party but with no place to go. Needless to say, they got their clocks cleaned in the 1980s.

Disinflation and tax reform stripped the subsidy effect from the ownership of tangible assets, which pulled out all the props from their high prices. As chart 2.9 on page 48 shows, the patterns of high returns on hard assets and low returns on securities, which had characterized the 1970s, was reversed during the 1980s. In the low-inflation 1980s, securities had high returns, and tangible assets were an anchor around your neck. Initially, skeptical investors, trained in the ways of the 1970s, refused to believe that times had changed and stubbornly clung to their hard assets. But as the evidence came in, month after month and year after year, that inflation really had been broken, investors' stubbornness began to crumble, and their asset demands began to change.

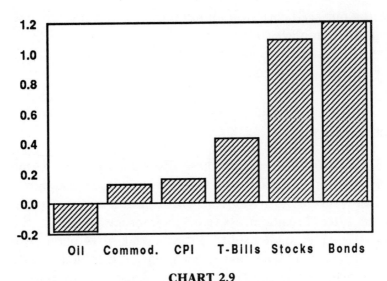

CHART 2.9
Asset Returns: 1982–1985

Blocks of farmland, mining deposits, and other hard assets were put up for sale in a market that didn't want them, and their prices began to fall. Falling hard asset prices led to further asset sales—more than $200 billion in 1985 by the Fortune 500 companies alone—and what began as a drop in inflation ended up in 1986 as *deflation*, an actual decline in prices. When the dust had settled, investors had reduced their holdings of tangible assets from a 1980 peak of 45 percent, back to 39 percent in 1987, as you can see in chart 2.6 on page 43. This $2 trillion drop in the demand to hold hard assets burst the balloon of pseudo–net worth built up during the 1970s and brought us back to earth with a resounding thud.

Falling hard asset prices in the 1980s eroded the collateral behind the loans the big banks had made to farmers, real estate developers, and Latin American governments, leading to massive loan defaults and scores of bank failures, as shown in chart 2.10. And falling hard asset prices put our companies through a decade of write-offs. Banks were forced to write off their bad loans. Oil and

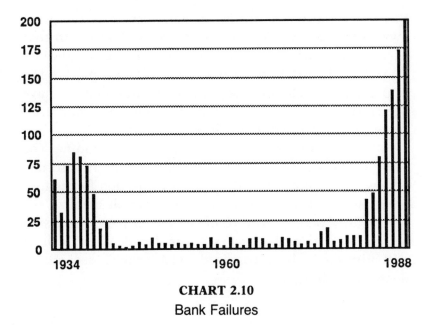

CHART 2.10
Bank Failures

mining companies were forced to write off the inflated values of their oil reserves and mineral deposits. And industrial companies were forced to write off the inflated values of the oil, gas, timber, mining, and real estate investments they had acquired during the 1970s. The hot air balloon of net worth that had made us all feel so good in the 1970s went up in flames like the *Hindenburg*, leaving many investors without a clue about what had gone wrong. Mark Twain may have come closest to capturing their emotions when he wrote in *Roughing It* about a similar experience that happened to him at the end of the Silver Rush:

> So vanished my dreams. So melted my wealth away. So toppled my airy castle to the earth and left me stricken and forlorn. Moralizing, I observed, then, that all that glitters is not gold. I can always have it to say that I was absolutely and unquestionably worth a million dollars once, for ten days.

But the deflation of the 1980s also served as the great
awakening. By stripping away the phony net worth that
was created by rising commodity prices, it exposed the fact
that we had allowed our stock of industrial capital to fall
into disrepair. The high real interest rates that we have
been forced to live with since that time, shown in chart 2.11,
serve as a measure of the scarcity of capital.

    This is not the end of the story; it's the beginning. The
real story of this book, as the remaining chapters describe,
is how the capital shortage has set in motion forces that
have already started to rebuild and reindustrialize the
American economy. The result will be a period of rising
prosperity with stable prices in the decade ahead, which
will ultimately be recognized as America's second industrial revolution.

Summary

The capital stock is crucial for determining our productivity, our income, and our standard of living. In the

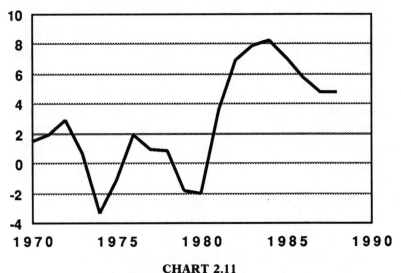

CHART 2.11
Real Interest Rates (%)

1970s, rising inflation, rising tax rates, and expanding tax shelters distorted the information and opportunities facing private investors, and seduced them into building the wrong stuff—hotels, office buildings, and shopping centers—instead of the factories and machines that we needed to maintain and strengthen our industrial base.

The resulting expansion of our measured net worth produced a false sense of euphoria that undermined work and savings, encouraged people to borrow, and led business managers to neglect the fundamentals of their businesses. In the end, we were hooked on inflation and tax shelters in the same way an addict is hooked on drugs. And like the drug addict, we were going to hell in a hand basket, but enjoying every minute of the ride.

In the 1980s, the joyride ended. The deflation and tax reform of the 1980s put American managers and investors through a cold-turkey withdrawal from our dependence on high inflation and tax shelters. That withdrawal stripped us of the false wealth created by high commodity prices, and forced us to write down the inflated values of our inflation hedges and tax shelters. It forced us to reevaluate our businesses, cut out portions that did not make sense, and refocus our efforts on making profits. And just like the drug addict going through withdrawal, it hurt like hell. Oil, farming, mining, and manufacturing all went through massive slumps that reverberated through the rest of the economy like the aftershocks following an earthquake.

But that withdrawal process also exposed our massive, cumulative shortage of industrial capital. That capital shortage, the aftermath of the roller-coaster inflation and deflation of the past twenty years, is the *real* cause of the pseudo-trends that people are so worried about today. And it has put forces into play that will ultimately bring about America's second industrial revolution.

3

Baby Boom to the Rescue

S EVENTY-SIX MILLION BABIES were born in the United States between 1946 and 1964, a performance unequaled in any other major country. This explosion of births distorted the American population distribution by creating an imbalance in the number of people in different age categories. Instead of having roughly similar numbers of people in each age category, as is typically the case, the Baby Boom created a bulge in the younger age categories, a change that has had a profound impact on U.S. economics and politics since the 1950s. The Baby Boomers brought us sit-ins, peace marches, and free love in the 1960s, made blue jeans chic, and propelled the Beatles to instant fame. Advertising campaigns that attempt to tie a particular product to the Baby Boom generation bear witness to the dominance of this group within the overall economy.

Two of the many changes in the American cultural and economic scenes credited to or blamed on the Baby Boom are the surge of credit card consumerism and the resultant decline in the savings rate during the past

twenty years. The lack of an adequate pool of savings to
tap for funds has retarded corporate investment spending
on new plant and equipment needed to keep pace with
international competition. As such, the Baby Boom bears
the brunt of the responsibility for the decline of American
competitiveness of recent years.

The lack of savings by Boomers has been explained in
a variety of ways. Some say the Vietnam War, which was
fought when the Boomers were in their late teens and
early twenties, produced a "live-for-today" attitude by
heightening the reality of death and bringing the fear of an
all-out war into such sharp focus. High inflation during
the Boomers' formative years (prices rose by a whopping
87 percent during the 1970s) is also used to explain the
"buy-today-before-the-price-goes-up" mentality. Interest
rate regulation, which held the price of credit artificially
low through the 1970s, meant that accelerating purchases
by borrowing to buy was even more advantageous. The
tax structure the Boomers first learned promoted debt,
too, by offering tax breaks on all forms of interest payments while simultaneously taxing the earnings on savings!

There is another explanation, however, for the so-
called profligacy of the Baby Boom generation that is
more compelling than those usually cited. The very existence of so large a group of relatively young people in the
economy almost ensures low savings because traditionally
people don't start saving until they reach their mid-forties
in any society or in any generation. The life-cycle theory
suggests that people spend more than they make through
about age thirty-five to thirty-nine. They then break even
for a few years before starting to accumulate funds for
their retirement by spending less than they make at about
age forty-five to forty-nine. Since the earliest group of
Baby Boomers has just reached their early forties, the
falling savings rate of recent years can be tied to this
life-cycle spending spree.

Inducements to spend rather than save, which have fueled Baby Boom borrowings up to now, are also beginning to change. Changes in tax laws that remove the deductibility of many interest payments and eliminate other shelters, together with continuing low inflation, will reduce the incentives to borrow and buy.

But most important the age composition of this generation is changing, too. Indeed, just like other folks, the Boomers get one year older every year, dragging the average age of our entire population up with them. As the Baby Boom ages, they will begin to confront the need to save for their retirement since most corporate pension plans are inadequate to sustain the life-style Boomers hope for in retirement. The grim prospects for the Social Security system, once the Boomers start to draw on it for their benefits, further enhance the need for private savings. Even before considering their own retirement, the Boomers have another major expense to face—educating their children. Soaring college tuition costs mean new parents need to start saving almost immediately if they hope to give their children a college education.

These changing economic incentives, and the changing age structure of the population, will raise the American savings rate during the next three decades. This turnaround will begin as a trickle of savings, but will become a flood by the year 2000, when the middle of the Baby Boom will be forty-five years old, and the oldest will be in their mid-fifties. Private savings generated by the Boomers, plus the huge surplus their tax payments will create in the Social Security trust fund while the Boomers work, will add trillions of dollars to domestic financial markets.

Increased source of domestic capital will reduce America's reliance on foreign money to finance industrial expansion. A higher savings rate will also help keep interest rates low, even if the federal budget deficit has not been eliminated. Slower growth in consumption will help to turn around America's trade deficit, because when people spend less in order to save more, they buy fewer of all types of goods, including imported products.

The danger of these otherwise positive developments, some economists would argue, is that a slowing trend in domestic consumption could mean slower growth in the economy, unless business spending or exports expand to take up the slack. So if the international economy is weak while the U.S. economy is undergoing this transformation from a consuming economy to a capital-spending economy, we could be in for a decade or more of slow growth. But history does not support these claims—Japan, Taiwan, Korea, and other high-savings countries are also the ones with the highest growth in income and living standards. As we discussed in chapter 2, accumulating capital, not spending money, is the key to long-term growth and prosperity.

The Baby Boom Changed the Shape of America

The Baby Boom was not a one-time surge in the number of babies born when American servicemen returned home from World War II. As you can see in chart 3.1, it was twenty years' worth of abnormally high birth rates, which lasted from the end of the war until the early 1960s. In 1946, nearly 4 million babies were born in the United States, 30 percent more than the number of births in 1944, just two years earlier, and the largest number of births in any year of the twentieth century up to that time. The number of babies born each year continued to grow almost without interruption to a peak of 4.3 million in 1960. By 1964, births decreased to 4 million per year and then continued to decline to a low of 3.1 million per year in 1971–1973.

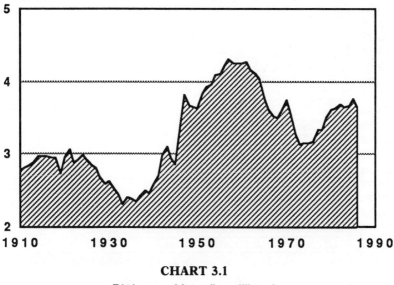

CHART 3.1
Births per Year (in millions)

As the number of babies born each year continued to rise, the profile of the American population by age category began to change. As chart 3.2 on page 58 shows, the age distribution in 1960 already showed the effects of the postwar jump in birth rates, in its enormous base of zero- to fourteen-year-olds. And all those zero- to fourteen-year-olds had to be fed, housed, clothed, and educated by the relatively small number of adults then working! But babies grow up to be young adults, as you can see in the tremendous bulge of twenty- to forty-year-olds—the Reebok, Perrier, BMW generation—in the 1986 population, shown in chart 3.3 on page 59.

More Teenagers Meant More Turbulence

This burst of births changed a lot more than the age distribution of the United States. It is one of the most important elements of social and political change in

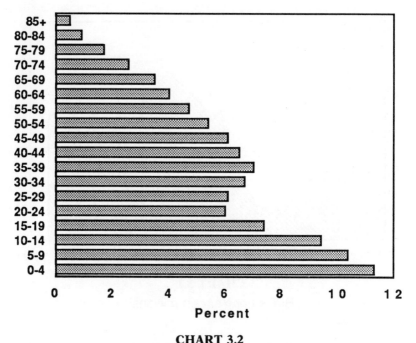

CHART 3.2

U.S. Age Structure: 1960

American culture and economics in this century. When the Boomers reached school age in the 1950s, they had no place to sit—so new classrooms and desks were built and new teachers were trained—reinforcing the trend toward more women in the work force to educate the Baby Boomers. The consumption patterns of this wave of teenagers in the early 1960s were felt across the country as record companies, clothing manufacturers, and others realized the massive potential market. Ford's Mustang, Levi's blue jeans, and Motown Records rode the wave of spending caused by this new group of consumers.

In the late 1960s, the country experienced the cultural turbulence brought about by the tidal wave of teenage Baby Boomers. College campuses were teeming with record numbers of students. New college facilities, seemingly built overnight to accommodate the demand, were overcrowded soon after they opened their doors. The

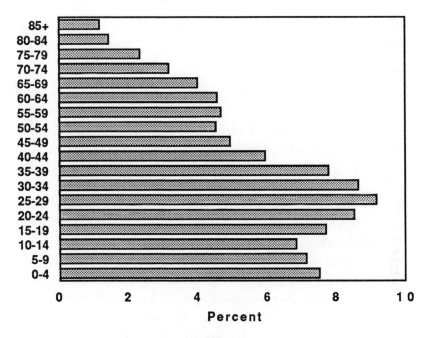

CHART 3.3
U.S. Age Structure: 1986

Vietnam War provided a focal point for this generation, which turned to campus violence, the peace movement, acid rock, and drugs to vent their frustrations.

Economically, the Boomers were well off because postwar expansion of the economy kept their parents employed. National income doubled from 1945 to 1956, and again by 1968. But when the large graduating classes began to look for work in the early 1970s, things did not look so rosy. As the jobs became harder to find, increasing demands were made on the government to provide employment and to keep the economy growing to absorb increasing numbers of workers. When hit by the oil price hikes of the 1970s, the economy reeled under the double effects of a deep recession and large numbers of new graduates seeking jobs. These pressures led to expansive government policies that helped to create the rapid inflation in the 1970s.

And Led to More Spending

The Boomers set up households and became self-supporting during the 1970s. Just as the goods producers had done before, the financial companies began to court these new customers. Credit card companies made mass mailings to graduating classes. Eager to have as rich a life-style as they had had with their parents, the Baby Boomers did not allow their new credit cards to gather dust. "Buy now, pay later" became the Baby Boomers' credo. Rising inflation made the strategy pay off for them. The deductibility of interest payments from taxable income made it seem as if they were getting something for nothing. Affordability was increasingly determined on the basis of cash flow—would your paycheck cover the monthly payment—rather than on wealth—did you have the money in the bank to pay for the item? And anyway, one could argue that he needed a color TV, stereo, nice

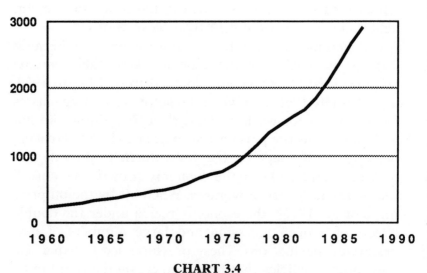

CHART 3.4
Consumer Debt (in billions$)

furniture, and clothes in order to make the right impression now, get the right job, and move up the corporate ladder as his father had done. The dramatic increase in the number of women college graduates—more women from the Baby Boom graduated from college than from any previous generation—meant more women deferring marriage for well-paid careers, increased numbers of new households being set up each year, and more spending on the items required to establish and maintain a household.

In the 1980s, the Boomers changed from Hippies to Yuppies. Long hair fell to the barbers' floors, turning former campus activists into advertising executives and investment bankers. Larger paychecks meant Baby Boomer families could afford bigger monthly payments on their house, their car, and other consumer goods. Consumer debt levels rose to unprecedented heights, as shown in chart 3.4, and the savings rate hit an all-time low of 2.8 percent of income in the fall of 1987, as shown in chart 3.5.

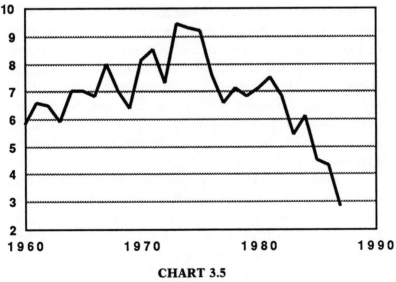

CHART 3.5

U.S. Savings Rate (%)

The Baby Boom Is Unique, but Boomer Behavior Is Not

The only thing that is unique about the Baby Boom is its size in proportion to the overall economy. The behavioral patterns of the Baby Boomers, from rebellious teenagers in the 1960s to profligate young adults in the 1980s, are typical of all generations (remember the Beatniks of the 1950s). But because there are so many Baby Boomers in relation to other age groups in the population, their behavior has dominated the economy.

The life-cycle theory of saving suggests that a person's spending patterns are largely determined by age, and that each individual's spending and savings habits will change in predictable ways as he grows older. A typical individual's income during his lifetime tends to follow a fairly predictable pattern, starting out low in the early years (childhood, starving student, and apprentice worker), rising to a peak in the thirties, forties, and fifties, then falling off again in retirement. Since people are aware of this pattern, the theory says, people will attempt to smooth out their spending patterns over their lifetimes by borrowing money to live beyond their income early in their lives, then saving large amounts out of their (higher) incomes later in life to pay off their debts and build a nest egg for retirement. This means a typical individual will go through two extended periods of dissaving, or negative savings—youth and retirement—and will do all of the saving he will do in his life during middle age, say between forty and sixty-five years.

Normally, in an economy where birth rates have been stable for some time, the high savers, who occupy the middle years of the population distribution, save more than enough to offset the dissaving done by the younger and older groups, and the society as a whole saves money. But if there is a surge in births, this natural balance is disturbed, and the abnormally large numbers of high-spending young people will show up as an abnormally low savings rate for the country as a whole. This is precisely what happened in the 1970s and 1980s when the free-spending Reebok, Perrier, and BMW generation celebrated its youth by wearing out its credit cards. There simply weren't enough high-saving gray hairs in the country to offset the Baby Boomers' behavior. But never fear, the Boomers are getting one year older every year. Just as the Boomers all joined hands to spend money during the 1970s and 1980s, they are going to turn into the most ferocious bunch of savers the world has ever seen in the 1990s. And that will turn a lot of currently accepted wisdom on its head.

The Parent Boom

After delaying the inevitable as long as they could, Baby Boomers are now leaving their carefree days as swinging singles and forming families. After entering the work force in record numbers and building successful careers, many Baby Boom women—who now average thirty-four years of age—have shifted to building families. Because of this, the number of births has climbed from a low of 3.1 million in 1972 through 1975 to a current level of 3.8 million.

As much as they would like to deny it, the Boomers are once again following traditional patterns, and are changing their life-styles to reflect their age. There are fewer nights out and more evenings spent in front of the big screen, playing a movie on the VCR and trying to forget the day at work. New parents are spending less of their money on themselves and more on their little darlings. So far, they are still spending money in a grand style to acquire the houses, furniture, household goods, and other trappings of middle-age, middle-class respectability. But it is just a matter of time before they finish feathering their nests and start to worry about the financial obligations that are going to descend on them as their little darlings begin to grow up.

In order for Baby Boomers to have a shot at achieving their aspirations for their children, they are going to have to save money, a lot of money, during the 1990s. The astronomical costs of educating the Boomers' children will force them to save, sooner or later. Private high schools and even elementary schools are more and more sought after by affluent Baby Boomers for their children. At present, private secondary schools cost an average of $5,000 per year for students who live at home. And the cost of getting a private college education is nearly $80,000. As chart 3.6 shows, students who will enter those same colleges and universities in the year 2000 just over ten years from now—the Baby Boomers' children—could face costs of $200,000 for the same degree. State universities, which now estimate the total cost of a four-year program to be about $28,000, could offer degrees with price tags of almost $80,000 by the turn of the century.

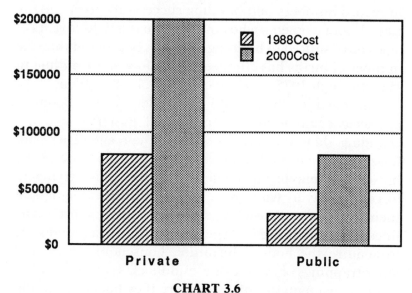

CHART 3.6

The Rising Costs of College Education

Faced with these crushing facts, even the most profligate Baby Boomers are going to realize they must save.
Many will feel they are saving in the form of accumulating
equity in their home, against which they plan to borrow
when funds are needed to make their children's tuition,
room, and board payments. That form of saving, however,
is only a way to delay paying the piper. Ultimately, the
home-equity loans will have to be repaid, so spending will
have to be reduced in future years. Of course, the prospect
of reducing spending in the future is more appealing to
most people than the idea of cutting back today. The
problem is that most Boomers are having their children so
late in life that if they delay saving for college too long,
they will not have much time left to accumulate a sufficient retirement nest egg for themselves.

Consider a couple who has two children two years
apart when the wife is thirty-four, and the husband is
thirty-nine. The first child will enter college when the
parents are fifty-two and fifty-seven. At an average annual
cost of nearly $20,000 per child for a state school, the
parents will spend $160,000 over the six years their
children are in college. By the time the last child graduates, the parents will be fifty-eight and sixty-three—too
late to pay off education debts and start saving for retirement.

The Retirement Time Bomb

Baby Boomers who are counting on Social Security payments to live on in their old age are going to be very
disappointed. As Boomers begin to retire in large numbers
in the early decades of the next century they will put
tremendous strains on both private and public retirement
programs. In the year 2025 (when Boomers will be all
retired but still jogging and drinking Perrier), there will be
only two working-age people for every retiree, compared

with ten-to-one in 1940 and five-to-one in 1980. Private pension plans are funded, meaning they are paid for, by setting aside enough dollars during a person's working days to meet the expected stream of benefits that that person will receive during retirement. But only about one-third of all workers are actually covered by pension plans, and for most of those who are covered, retirement benefits will amount to less than 20 percent of their preretirement incomes.

Worse yet, the Social Security system is not funded in the same manner as private pension plans. Rather, it is a "hand-to-mouth" system, where the money collected from workers today is immediately spent to pay benefits to people who are now retired. Thus, your retirement income is not determined by the amount of money you pay into the system; it is determined by the amount that can be collected from the guy who will still be working at the point you retire. If he won't pay, you won't eat. This won't be a problem for the next several years. Between now and 2020, there will be so many Boomers working and paying Social Security taxes that they will be paying in much more than today's retirees will draw out, so the system will build a massive surplus—a stockpile of government bonds—on which it can draw when the Boomers retire. However, the surplus will quickly be drawn down once the Boomers start to draw their benefits in the next century and could be bankrupt by the year 2050. Since there are so many Baby Boomers, and since there are so few people coming through the age distribution just after them, smart Baby Boomers should be asking themselves where their dinner is going to come from when they retire.

Social Security checks today provide little more than one-quarter of a retiree's income. The rest is provided by part-time earnings, income from investments, and private retirement plans. And Social Security benefits account for a smaller share of total income for those who have begun receiving benefits since mid-1980 than for older retirees.

Baby Boomers will begin to draw from the Social Security system in 2010, and their withdrawals will peak in 2020. It is estimated by Boskin and Puffert of the National Bureau of Economic Research that an individual born in 1945 will lose between $27,000 and $44,000 of the payments they made to the system while they were working. In other words, they will be able to draw far less out than they put in, after accounting for the rate of return they could have earned on their Social Security contributions if they had been allowed to simply put it in a savings account. For higher-income individuals, the situation is worse. While low-income individuals will receive approximately sixty cents of benefits per dollar of earned income while they were working, high-income individuals will receive only an average of twenty-six cents on the dollar. Single recipients fare even worse because they do not receive spousal benefits. These figures are for early Boomers, born in 1945. Those born in the later stages of the Baby Boom and post-Boomers born in the 1970s face the prospect of a bankrupt Social Security system by the year 2050.

The Role of Personal Savings

Any retirement income over that provided by Social Security or a private pension plan must come from personal savings. As an example, consider a couple who desires a retirement income of $30,000 annually. Based on current averages, they will receive a monthly Social Security benefit of about $483, or $5,803 annually. Average private pension benefits are $400 a month or $4,800 a year. So the couple needs to save enough during their working lives to provide an additional $1,671 per month, or $19,397 per year, in retirement earnings if they want to achieve their goal. At an interest rate of 8 percent, this means they must amass an investment portfolio of $242,462 during their working lives. A single retiree receives an average Social Security benefit of only $260 per month, so even with a private pension comparable to that of the couple above, he or she will need to add an extra $33,450 to savings to generate the additional income needed to meet an annual income target of $30,000.

It is not certain, of course, that future retirees will be able to earn 8 percent on their savings. Many older persons today have watched their monthly income fall by two-thirds or more since 1981 while interest rates on money market funds fell from 18 percent to today's levels. If interest rates average 6 percent, instead of 8 percent, the above couple would need a savings account of $323,270 to generate the $19,397 gap in retirement income left by the shortfall in Social Security and pension payments.

And these projections are, if anything, optimistic. Faced with the huge payout looming in 2020 and beyond, there is a good chance that the Social Security system will be amended to reduce or eliminate payments to upper-income Boomers. In that case, a couple receiving private pension benefits of $400 per month, but with no Social Security payments, would need a nest egg of $420,000 invested at 6 percent to generate a total retirement income of just $30,000. Those without private pension resources will need savings of $500,000 just to live modestly!

Economic Incentives to Save Are Improving

The Boomers' penchant for overconsumption and debt was a reasonable response to high inflation and tax breaks on interest payments. But these incentives to borrow and buy are no longer with us nearly to the extent they used to be. During the 1970s, inflation accelerated from 3 percent to 14 percent, driving the prices of housing and other "inflation hedges" higher. The average price of a single-family home doubled during the decade of the 1970s.

When this was purchased with 80 percent borrowed money, as is typical, an owner's equity increased by ten times. Meanwhile, the interest paid on the mortgage was deducted from taxable income, which means that up to 70 percent of the interest payments for purchasing a house were paid by the government. This made housing the best investment by far for the average person in the 1970s. Under these conditions, it made sense to purchase other goods on credit as well, items such as cars and washing machines, which are not expected to appreciate but which do provide a stream of service value to their owner. Purchasing goods whose value went up at about the same rate as interest meant that there was effectively little or no interest penalty at all. And since the interest payments were deductible, the buyer often actually made money on the purchase.

By comparison, almost every form of *financial* savings lost value in the 1970s. Savings accounts were constrained by regulation to pay an interest rate of only 4.5 percent. Since prices were going up by an average of 7.5 percent per year, anyone who put their money in a savings account *lost* an average of 3 percent per year on their money. Government bonds fared even worse. An investor who purchased long-term bonds at 8 percent in 1975 lost half their value by 1980. And the total return of the stock market (including dividends and capital gains) was 11.3 percent lower than the increase in the price level for the same period. So, to paraphrase Alfred E. Newman, the Boomers developed the attitude of "What, me save?"

However, during the past eight years, inflation has fallen from 14 percent to 3.5 percent and hit as low a rate as 1.1 percent in 1986. The prices of many products, including televisions, computers, cars, and watches have actually come down or risen by less than the overall price level. Housing prices began to rise again in 1986, but they declined or were stable in most parts of the country from 1981 through 1985. In addition, the top tax rate on income was cut from 70 percent to 33 percent, slicing the advantage to borrowing funds for buying houses roughly in half. Credit card interest and interest on all but primary residences and second homes are no longer deductible. Meanwhile, capital gains are now taxed as ordinary income, further reducing the advantages of buying homes for profit. These changes have made housing an expense again, rather than the no-brainer investment it was during the inflation binge of the 1970s.

During the same eight years when many products' prices declined and housing prices were stable, the value of stocks and bonds more than doubled—even taking into account the crash of October 1987. Because of this, these types of investments have gained in popularity. One in four households now owns stocks through a mutual fund, compared to one in eight households in 1980. In 1987, private investors poured $15 billion per month into government bonds. Times and investment strategies have certainly changed.

Inflation in the coming decade should remain under control. Factories are being built and improvements in productivity are being made to allow these factories to produce goods with less labor and raw materials and lower costs than ever before. These increases in capacity and efficiency mean plenty of goods will be available at stable prices into the foreseeable future. Even a doubling of oil prices in 1987, and a 50 percent decline of the dollar from 1985 to 1987, pushed inflation to only 4.5 percent in 1987.

The future course of U.S. tax policy is less certain. The federal budget deficit will keep the political heat on the White House to raise tax revenues. But George Bush's famous campaign promise not to raise income tax rates means that any increases in tax rates will likely be limited to gasoline, cigarettes, alcohol, and other specialty taxes, which could actually *promote* savings by reducing the consumption of the taxed items. And it is highly unlikely

that any of the old exemptions, such as credit card interest
or expenses on passive investments, would be restored by
a Congress that is intent on raising revenue. We could even
see the return of the broad-based Individual Retirement
Account (IRA) and increased limits on the amounts that
can be set aside in pension plans designed for the self-
employed and those working for small companies, specif-
ically Keogh and 401-K plans.

Altogether, future economic and tax incentives will
favor a higher savings rate. Combined with the aging of
the population to where the biggest age groups will be in
their prime saving phase for the next thirty years, lower
inflation and taxes and fewer tax breaks for debt will help
to push U.S. savings back up to its historical average of 8
to 10 percent of our incomes.

The Magnitude of New Savings

In 1987 Americans saved a pathetic 3.7 percent of their
after-tax income (approximately $120 billion). This in-
cludes only savings that went into private bank accounts
or into stocks or bonds. It does not include pension
contributions, additions to IRAs or other retirement plans,
or increased equity in homes. If the savings rate had been
8 percent, the average for the postwar period, we would
have pumped an *additional* $180 billion—for a total of
$300 billion—into the country's financial markets, instead
of using the money to purchase goods. At a 10 percent
savings rate we would have pumped $400 billion in funds
into stocks, bonds, bank accounts, and money market
accounts, an increase of $280 billion over the actual levels
recorded in 1987. American households are worth about
$15 trillion, today, if you add up all their holdings of
financial assets, real estate, commodities, and the like,
according to the Federal Reserve Board's *Balance Sheet of
the United States*. About 60 percent of this, or $8.6 trillion,

is held in the form of financial instruments, the remainder being hard assets such as real estate and goods. A return to a savings rate of 10 percent, assuming an interest rate on investments of 8 percent, would add $3 trillion to this total in one decade, $7.5 trillion in twenty years, and nearly $15 trillion in thirty years, including compound interest of 8 percent. This would double the net worth of America's households by the year 2020 when the Boomers begin to retire in large numbers.

Faced with the staggering size of savings balances needed to generate even a modest retirement income, and tax and economic conditions more favorable to savings than in the past, the Boomers have no alternative than to save money. And the sooner the better. The average Boomer is now thirty-five years old. If a person saves just $7,000 a year from that age until he is sixty-five, and invests at 8 percent, he will accumulate $323,000, which would give him an income of $30,000 per year in retirement. If he waits until age fifty-five to start saving, he will need to put aside nearly $25,000 per year to achieve the same goal.

Will There Be Any Bonds Left to Buy?

In 1983, Congress enacted legislation that substantially amended the Social Security system. They raised contribution rates, delayed cost-of-living adjustments, extended coverage to more workers, extended the normal retirement age, and made other changes intended to improve the financial health of the system. Under current projections incorporating those changes, the Trust Fund will run a surplus—it will take in more money than it pays out each year—for the next forty years. During this period the Social Security Trust Fund will accumulate nearly $12.5 trillion in assets before expenses again exceed inflow in 2030! Most Baby Boomers have already entered the active work force. This means that 120 million Baby Boomers are now paying taxes, but only about 36 million retired and disabled persons are collecting benefits. This situation will change dramatically as the Baby Boomers near retirement age. In 2030, when there will be only two workers per retiree, the system will begin to run large annual deficits until it is exhausted in 2050. Nonetheless, over the next forty years this huge buildup of funds will provide a tremendous source of capital to be invested in U.S. financial markets.

To be sure, one of the obvious questions facing those responsible for investing this money will be where to put it. Even under the most pessimistic assumptions, the government debt will not exceed $6 trillion. Since the Social Security surplus could be as high as $12 trillion, at least $6 trillion will have to be invested in private securities, such as corporate and municipal bonds or stocks. The government could unintentionally become a controlling shareholder of large corporations as it is forced to keep investing these funds. Unfortunately, we cannot be certain that Congress will have the willpower to keep its fingers out of the cookie jar—they may decide to tap the Social Security till for favorite programs when it starts to overflow.

From Capital Shortage to Plenty

The shift from consumption to saving that will accompany the maturing of the Baby Boomers in the 1990s will provide the funds to help us build our way out of the capital shortage that has plagued this country for the last twenty years. As discussed in chapter 2, our shortage of modern, efficient industrial capital was caused by distortions to the incentives to accumulate capital due to high inflation, high tax rates, and tax shelters. It made sense for people to spend, not save, and to devote what scarce savings there were to building inflation and tax shelters, not industrial capital. And the Baby Boomers' adolescent spending frenzy only worsened the problem by further reducing our pool of savings. But in the 1990s, a shift toward savings by the Baby Boomers will create a larger pool of investable capital; changed economic conditions and high rates of return produced by the shortage itself will motivate the flow of this capital into the rebuilding of America's industrial base.

The estimates that have been presented here suggest that the pool of private savings could grow by as much as $15 trillion over the next thirty years. In addition, the Social Security Trust Fund has the potential to add another $12.5 trillion. Together, this $27.5 trillion of financial investments will provide American companies with a flood of new capital between today and 2020!

Still, this turnaround will not be sudden. The early Baby Boomers are just beginning to enter their forties. It will be ten years before the entire herd of Baby Boomers have been rounded up and firmly locked into their prime saving years. But the trickle has already begun. There are already signs that savings may have bottomed and are beginning to turn the corner. From an all-time low of 2.8 percent in late 1987, the savings rate rebounded to over 4 percent in 1988. Curiously, the crash in the stock market in October 1987 may be responsible for kicking off this turnaround, both because it may have convinced investors that the government can't protect them from all economic worries, and by actually reducing their net worth. Since people save in order to build an investment balance big enough to allow them to live off its interest during their retirement years, a reduction in net worth—due to the stock market decline—means people will have to save more in the future to offset the losses. The investment house of Bear Stearns has estimated that an additional five cents will be saved every year in the future for every dollar lost in the crash as investors get down to work rebuilding their wounded portfolios. This will amount to an increase in new savings of $40 billion in 1988 alone.

By 1995, the savings rate should be back to 6 percent, and 10 percent by 2000, with most of the gain caused by the aging of the Baby Boomers. As chart 3.7 shows, the Japanese population today is significantly "older" than the U.S. population, i.e., their people are heavily concentrated in the forty to sixty age groups, compared with our concentration in the Baby Boom years. This could explain a portion of the glaring difference in the savings rates of the two countries. By the year 2000, however, the age structure in the United States should be almost an exact duplicate of today's age structure in Japan. While cultural differences and differences in the way our two governments measure savings suggest our savings rate will not equal Japan's current rate of 16 percent, the life-cycle hypothesis indicates that even 10 percent is a modest projection.

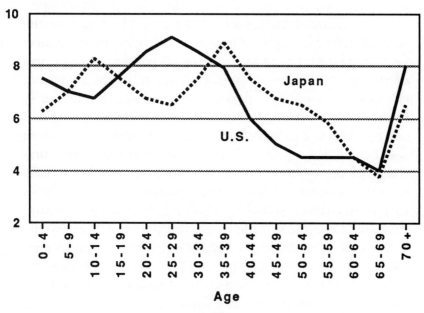

CHART 3.7

Current U.S. and Japanese Age Structures (in millions)

More Savings Will Restore Health to Financial Markets

More savings will mean healthier financial markets in the 1990s. Stock and bond markets are the avenues through which funds are channeled into new factories, machinery, and other capital goods. The savings of individual investors provide the funds borrowed by corporations and entrepreneurs to build new businesses. In a healthy financial market with an ample supply of funds, this process works smoothly to the benefit of investors and borrowers alike. Even funds invested in bank accounts add to the capital stock by giving banks the money to make business loans to companies seeking to expand their capacity or renovate their existing facilities.

When more funds are made available to the markets from domestic sources through increased savings, the dependence on foreign money is reduced. Presently, the U.S. government bond market is highly dependent upon foreign investors. Foreigners own about 15 percent of the federal government's outstanding debt, and in recent years have purchased as much as 40 percent of each new debt offering. When, for reasons determined by their own economy or tax policy, they decide not to participate fully in our market, our interest rates are buffeted about, and our markets are shaken. Today investors anxiously wait to see if the Japanese trust banks and life insurance companies will be big buyers at government securities auctions in order to get an idea of whether interest rates will have to rise to attract sufficient demand. Increased domestic savings of the magnitude discussed above will allow the U.S. markets to shake free of this dependence on foreign money by sometime in the mid-1990s. Foreign money will still be a welcome addition to the market, but it will not have the dominant influence it has today.

Further, a higher savings rate helps keep interest rates low. Interest rates, like other prices, are set by supply and demand. When the demand for funds rises because corporations are borrowing to finance acquisitions and expansions, or because the government is running budget deficits, there is pressure on interest rates to go up unless the supply of funds into the debt market also expands. In the early and mid-1970s the U.S. government attempted to keep interest rates low by printing new money and using those dollars to buy its own securities when they were issued. This type of "printing press" finance does not keep interest rates low, as we learned the hard way. It leads to inflation, which causes interest rates to rise instead of fall. For interest rates to remain stable or fall in the face of increased demand for credit, the increase in the supply of funds must come from the private sector, such as through increased savings.

In the early 1980s, the U.S. bond market benefited from an increased supply of funds from private sources, allowing interest rates to fall substantially, even as the government budget deficit swelled. Due to the dramatic drop in the inflation rate, individuals saw that housing and commodities, the inflation hedges in which they had invested so feverishly in the 1970s, were not likely to rise much in price. Interest-bearing bonds looked much more attractive, so people and companies sold their hard assets to invest in bonds and stocks. All told, more than $1 trillion moved into the stock and bond markets out of hard assets. Interest rates fell from double to single digits, and inflation remained moderate, despite the dire predictions of those who thought increased government deficits had to mean higher inflation and interest rates. Their error was not recognizing the difference made by the source of the money to finance the deficit.

In the 1990s and into the twenty-first century, financial markets will again benefit from an inflow of money from private savings. Sure, controlling the government deficit matters, but more for the purpose of using funds productively than for determining the course of interest rates. As we discussed above, an increase in the savings rate to 8 percent will add about $200 billion to the supply of funds each year. So unless the deficit grows by more than that, interest rates will tend to decline.

More Productive Investments

Lower interest rates and healthier financial markets encourage more productive investments by corporations. When a company is deciding whether to put up a new factory or retool an old one by switching to modern machinery, its managers compare the return they expect to receive on the new facilities with the cost of raising the money to make the change. Many projects do not make economic sense if they are going to have to pay 12 or 15 percent for money, but would be profitable at a cost of 9 or 10 percent. One of the reasons Japan has so much modern equipment is that companies are able to borrow at 4 or 5 percent due to their ample savings and low inflation rate. So more savings in the United States will add to the amount of new equipment and machinery, which will help to make our industry competitive again.

Higher Productivity and Wages

Higher productivity growth is the biggest payoff to higher savings and investment. Increased savings, by adding to the rate of capital formation, will also help to raise the productivity of American workers and the competitiveness of American industry by giving our workers better tools to do their jobs. And higher productivity means a higher standard of living. The more productive each worker is, the more he can be paid and still leave a reasonable profit margin for the corporation to reward its investors and lenders. And the faster productivity grows, the more competitive American industry can be.

The Trade Deficit

Higher savings rates will help turn the trade deficit around in two ways: by reducing the demand for imports and by helping American producers to sell more abroad. Saving more means spending less on both domestic and imported goods—Americans now import more than 10 percent of the goods we consume. So some of the reduced spending will lower our import bill. In addition, increased investment and enhanced productivity brought on by more savings will reduce our manufacturing costs and make American-made products more competitive, helping American producers to win consumers back from foreign competitors in our own market and to sell more abroad as well. The miracle economies of the postwar years, including those of Germany, Japan, Korea, and Taiwan, have all built their export successes on massive capital investment. Increased investment in the United States will allow American producers to reap the same rewards.

Savings

The cost of increased savings is reduced consumption. Every additional penny saved is a penny not used to purchase a home, a washing machine, or some other consumer product. Consumption spending is over 60 percent of the national income in America, as in most other industrial countries. So a sudden cutoff of consumer spending would leave a lot of unsold products on retailers' shelves, lead to widespread layoffs, and push the economy into a sharp recession. But the same forces that are tending to depress consumer spending in the next decade will also mean rapid growth of spending on capital goods and exports. The key to keeping the economy growing is for these changes to take place smoothly, over a long period of time.

4

The Trade Deficit:
It's OK, We're OK

THE TRADE DEFICIT, according to many politicians and economists, is the Darth Vader of the American economy. It exports high-paying manufacturing jobs to low-wage countries and threatens to impoverish our children by making us the biggest debtor nation in the world. Critics say the trade deficit, which totaled $171 billion in 1987, must be cut at any cost by raising taxes and erecting tariff barriers to discourage Americans from buying foreign goods and by punishing those foreign countries, such as Japan and Taiwan, that don't buy as many U.S. products as we would like. But the United States does not have a trade problem, it has a capital problem, and Darth Vader may actually turn out to be our friend.

As we discussed in chapter 2, the U.S. economy produced and invested in "the wrong stuff"—hotels, office buildings, shopping centers, and other unproductive assets—during the last twenty years, instead of the industrial plants and capital equipment we needed to compete internationally. Now, after writing off all of this wrong stuff during the 1980s, we find ourselves without much stuff at all, just like a developing country, with more workers than there are tools for them to use. After all, there is very little practical difference between an old, inefficient factory that has been closed down and no factory at all. Now that the wreckage of the inflationary 1970s has been cleared away, however, the stage is set for the reindustrializing of the largest, most politically stable, and richest developing country in the history of the world. It is going to be quite a show.

But rebuilding an entire economy, especially one the size of America's, takes real money. We need the money to finance the people and resources to build new equipment and modernize and replace America's worn-out factories. Unfortunately, we don't have it. Big-spending Baby Boomers and a bloated government budget mean that we have not saved much in the past decade, nor are we currently generating sufficient funds to finance redevelopment on our own. Chapter 3 argued that an enormous jump in savings rates should take place in the 1990s, when the Baby Boomers learn that they too are subject to the law of gravity and must save the money to educate their children and finance their retirement years. But we can't hold our breaths waiting for the Boomers to get started; it's going to be a while. We need a jump start to get our economic engines running at full speed, and we need it now.

Getting a capital-short, developing country to grow is a very difficult problem. To grow you must have ample supplies of tools for your workers. But you can only produce tools out of your current savings. And people can't save much because their incomes are low because they don't have the tools to produce competitive products. Germany and Japan were trapped in that vicious circle after the war, when their industrial capital had been leveled by Allied bombers. If they had been forced to do it with domestic savings alone, it would have taken a lifetime to rebuild their shattered economies. There was simply no production and income to save. But both countries were able to break out of the vicious circle of low capital, low income, low savings by getting their dead batteries jump started from a capital-rich America through the Marshall Plan and the massive flow of private American capital that accompanied it in the late 1940s and 1950s.

Fortunately, we are not alone today. There are several foreign countries, including Japan, Germany, and Taiwan, that have built up enormous stockpiles of capital goods and are saving lots of money. These high-savings countries produce money surpluses over and above their own domestic investment needs each year, surpluses that have to be invested somewhere. International capital flows allow us to borrow their excess funds to finance our development, and they allow foreign investors to earn higher rates of return than they could receive in their home markets. The trade deficit is the mechanism by which foreign investors earn dollars to invest here; without the trade deficit, there could be no injection of foreign funds, and we would have to do it the hard way.

This process of running a trade deficit in order to borrow from your neighbors has a long tradition among the industrial countries of the world. In fact, it is how they were built in the first place. Several centuries ago, the British Industrial Revolution was financed with capital that was borrowed largely from the Dutch. During the nineteenth and early twentieth centuries, the United States built the strongest industrial country in the world with funds borrowed from England, Holland, and Germany. In this century, the economic miracles of Japan and Germany, after the war, and Korea after them, were financed primarily by American loans. In fact, most major industrial countries of today borrowed from abroad to finance the development of their manufacturing sectors at sometime in their histories.

Countries that have tried to go it alone or boot-strap

their way to growth or that have been too politically unstable for private investors to risk their capital have met with limited or no success. The Soviet Union, for example, lags far behind the level of output and income per capita of most free-world industrial economies that have had the benefit of foreign borrowings. China has now discovered that even her huge natural resource of over 1 billion people cannot create a modern economy without injections of foreign capital.

Some observers compare the United States' current international debt to that of Mexico and Brazil. They claim that the money we are borrowing is being spent on consumer goods and frivolous government expenditures, and that as a result we will not be able to repay it when the loans come due. While it is true that the low savings rates and large budget deficits of the 1980s acted as a drain on national savings and capital formation, the trade account itself has been a valuable source of new capital. A close look at these accounts reveals that more than half of the deterioration in the U.S. trade position in the 1980s was attributable to increased imports of capital ma- chinery and industrial materials. These capital goods are resources, not products, and will be used to produce goods for many years in the future. A piece of productive capital equipment represents higher future output and living standards. That future output, however, is wrapped in a package and tied with a ribbon that can only be untied by an American worker, so more capital equipment means more jobs too. It is the marriage of the worker and his tools that creates value. Ultimately, we will repair our trade imbalance and repay our debts by using the new capital goods to produce here at home much of what we now import, and to export competitive products to the rest of the world.

Those who denounce trade deficits as exporting jobs and mortgaging our children's future must not be able to count. The United States has created 15 million jobs since

1980, more than Europe has created in the past quarter century. Due to the increased supply of modern capital equipment made possible by the trade deficit, American manufacturing productivity is soaring, and our costs of production are now lower than in most other developed countries, as we will show later in this chapter. These changes will enable us to produce and sell more products in the future, and eventually stop borrowing and repay our debts. And remember that foreign countries, companies, and individuals have debts to U.S. investors, too; it was American capital that financed their industrial expansion after the war. Since our net earnings from international investments in 1987 were actually in the black, it's hard to believe that we are floundering in debt. How can we be a debtor and a creditor at the same time?

When politicians, in their snake-oil speeches, lament that the United States is the biggest debtor nation in the world, as the "official" statistics showed at the end of 1987, they are using "voodoo" accounting. The official numbers they rely on are measured at book value, which is basically the historical cost of making an investment at the time it was made, less charges for depreciation. But the tidal wave of U.S. investment abroad took place between 1946 and the mid-1960s, when prices were much lower. This means that a building purchased by an American investor in Paris for $10,000 in 1951, and used ever since as their overseas office, will still be carried on the books at $10,000, minus the amount they have taken as depreciation over the years, even though the building today might be worth $2 million. So the value of U.S. investments abroad is grossly understated in the official statistics. In contrast, most of the foreign investments that people are so worried about today were made in the 1980s, and their book values will be much closer to their actual values in the market at current prices. When attempts are made to correct for this book value distortion to the official figures, revised estimates suggest that the United States is actually still a net creditor. This makes sense, since as mentioned above we enjoy positive net income from international investments.

A country's books, just like a family's checkbook, must always be in balance. If a family spends more than it earns, it has to get the money from somewhere, usually the bank. And when a family makes an investment that its savings are not large enough to cover, such as a new home, it borrows the money. But being in debt does not necessarily mean the family is guilty of bad financial management; it means they decided to buy a house and to devote some portion of their future income to paying it off while they are using it. The same is true for a country. If a country spends more on imports than it earns by selling exports, it must run a deficit on its trade account. This requires an exactly matching flow of funds coming in from abroad, in the form of loans and investments, which is referred to as a surplus on the capital account. So the trade deficit is just the flip side of the capital inflow—you can't have one without the other. Whether or not the transaction makes sense depends on whether the capital will be used to finance productive investment, which will produce enough income in the future to repay the loans, and on whether domestic savings will eventually increase by enough to take over the funding of industry. While Baby Boomers will begin to save in a big way in the middle of the 1990s, we have to choose between foreign funds and no funds until then. But how *are* current borrowings from abroad being used?

Advance Orders for Future Goods

"Politics," H. L. Mencken wrote, "is the advance auction of stolen goods." Trade deficits are advance orders for future exports. By putting their money into the U.S.

economy today, foreign investors are essentially saying, "Here's my cash, I'll take two of those widgets when they are ready in 1995." This is because the only way that foreign investors can ever take their money home is in the form of American-made products. Someday, foreign investors will want to cash in their U.S. investments to support their standard of living back home. When this happens they will buy more from abroad than they sell, and run a trade deficit. And their trade deficit is our trade surplus. The unavoidable implication is that American exporters are going to sell a lot of product in the 1990s.

Think of it this way. Suppose you were the owner of a hamburger stand whose business had been a little slow. In order to stimulate additional sales, you ran a special and gave out a certificate for one burger and an order of fries to every customer who bought a burger during the month of June. Now after the special is over, you know that somewhere out there on the streets of Mudville there are 340 gift certificates in people's pockets. Your fondest hope, of course, is that all 340 of those people would get run over by a bus, and their gift certificates would be quietly buried in their pockets. That's not very likely to happen, however, either in Mudville or in the international accounts. Someday your customers are going to show up, shove the certificates under your nose, and expect to eat dinner. And when they do, you're going to be frying up a lot of burgers.

In exactly the same way, when foreign investors decide it's time to pick up their marbles and go home, American exporters are going to be frying up a lot of exports. And just as the United States had to run a trade deficit in order to get the money into the country, we are going to have to run a trade surplus to get it back out again when our foreign creditors decide they want their money. In this way, the current trade deficits and the building of international debts in the United States are really stockpiles of orders for American-made goods.

Trade Deficits and Capital Flows

In order to understand the symmetry between what are
called the *trade* and *capital* accounts, it is useful to review
the basics of international accounting. A country's balance
of payments summarizes all the transactions between
residents of that country and the rest of the world. There
are three parts to the balance of payments. The first part is
the *trade balance.* In this portion of the accounts, the
proceeds of all of the goods that a country sells abroad
(exports) are tallied as revenue, and the costs of the goods
imported from abroad are counted as expenses. A trade
surplus is recorded when you export more goods than you
import, and a deficit when more goods are imported than
exported.

The second part of the international accounts is the
service account balance, which works like the trade balance except that it deals with intangible services such as
insurance, shipping, and interest payments. Adding together the trade balance and the service account balance
produces the *current account* balance—the sum of tangible
and intangible goods and services.

The third part is the *capital account,* which records
transactions between countries in assets such as stocks,
bonds, and deposits. If foreigners purchase more U.S.
Treasury bonds than we purchase of their securities, for
example, we will record a net inflow of funds—a surplus in
our capital account. While it sounds good to be bringing in
more money than you are sending out, the money is not
coming in for free. If foreigners are buying our Treasury
bonds, we must pay their money back at some point, with
interest. So, unlike the current account where money is
earned from the sale of goods and services, money brought
in through the capital account must be repaid, implying a
future expense.

Here comes the trick. Since the country's books must

balance, the current account must balance with the capital account at all times. If a country is importing more than it exports, so that it has a current-account deficit, it must be borrowing the money from abroad by running a capital-account surplus, in other words by issuing IOUs to foreigners.

Trade Deficits Can Result from Too Little Savings

The reason generally given for the current U.S. trade deficit is that American consumers are on a buying binge of foreign goods, produced with cheap labor, while foreign consumers are prevented from buying more of our goods by discriminatory trade restrictions imposed by their governments. However, since the trade deficits are just the flip side of capital surpluses, it is just as accurate to say that we have a trade deficit because we have a shortage of savings.

When a country that has been running a capital-account surplus and trade deficit no longer needs money from abroad, due to a sudden reduction of either government or corporate spending or to an increase in its savings rate, the country may suddenly be saving more than it needs. It will then want to export this capital abroad where it may earn a higher return. This means the capital surplus must turn to a deficit, and the trade deficit must turn to surplus. South Korea is such a case. Up until 1985, Korea was the third largest international debtor in the world. Then, almost overnight, Korea's massive investments in heavy industry began to pay off, and exploding Korean exports began to generate more money than Korean firms required for further investment. The Koreans began early repayment of their debt and ran their first-ever trade surplus in 1986. Ironically, Korea has been attacked in the U.S. Congress for its success in selling consumer goods in the United States. Congress would like to restrict Korean exports and force them to spend more on American products. Yet, most of the $35 billion in debts that Korea accumulated during the period they were importing U.S. capital goods to build up their industrial base is owed to American banks. Clearly, if someone owes you money, it is not a good idea to try and throw him out of work.

Of course, whether a country is ever able to repay its debts depends on whether the money was used wisely to build new industrial operations or was squandered on current consumption. The United States, in the late 1800s, and present-day Japan and Korea are prime examples of countries that used borrowed funds wisely. Mexico, on the other hand, is a country that is now suffering under the burden of debt repayment with little additional productive capacity to help it make the payments.

Case History: Japan

From the end of the war until the late 1950s, Japan ran the largest trade deficit in the world. Then, in spite of predictions that the quality of their products was too low for them ever to become a major exporter, the Japanese trade account turned to surplus in 1964. In the 1980s, they have had the largest trade surpluses in the world. This did not take place due to luck or unfair trading practices, but because Japan used the funds provided by its early trade deficits to import the capital goods to build a massive industrial base, which made their current trade surpluses possible.

Three important lessons for America can be drawn from the Japanese experience. First, Japan radically changed its mix of imports during its deficit years. It, too, started out by importing goods to be consumed. Food was Japan's biggest import item for many years after the war.

Second, without imports, Japan's drive to industrialize would have failed. They imported the raw materials for their textile industries during the 1950s and 1960s, crude oil to fire their plants, and scrap iron and steel to build factories and machines. In the later stage of their deficit period, Japan also imported substantial amounts of machines and other modern capital equipment. Third, their trade deficit period was characterized by investment, restructuring, and modernization. Investments were modest at first, but accelerated as the profits from early investments were plowed back into further expansion. In the early 1950s, the capital stock grew by only 3.8 percent per year. By the late 1950s, this number was up to 6.7 percent. It passed 10 percent in the early 1960s, and 13 percent in the 1970s. In comparison, the capital stock growth rates of the United States (3.5 percent) and Germany (5.5 percent) seem quite small.

This high rate of capital expansion in the later periods was made possible by increasing savings. After the war, Japan's gross private savings rate—including both personal and business saving—was 18 percent, roughly equal to the U.S. figure. But by 1960, Japan's gross private savings rate had jumped to 27 percent. The government helped, too, by making cheap funds available to strategic industries and promoting industrialization through tax concessions. Scarce capital meant high returns for investors, who plowed their winnings back into new ventures. Low inflation, steady economic policy, and the freedom to import capital where it was needed were added spurs to investment.

When Japan's exports began to surge in the 1960s, their trade deficit turned to surplus. Most notable is that they accomplished this entirely without a reduction in imports. The ability to export, not artificial restraints on imports, was the key to the Japanese success story.

Case History: Korea

South Korea ran a trade deficit in every year of postwar history until 1986. All at once, the Korean trade deficit flipped to a $4 billion surplus, and then doubled to $8 billion in 1987. From being the world's fourth largest debtor in 1985, Korea is now on the road to joining Japan and Taiwan as one of the world's creditors. The Korean experience shows even more dramatically than that of Japan how capital imports can be used to reindustrialize an entire economy.

When the Korean war ended in 1953, South Korea had no money and very little machinery. It survived, living hand-to-mouth, on concessional loans and foreign aid provided by the United States. Then, in the early 1970s, Korea embarked on a program to build an industrial base using funds borrowed from abroad and imported capital equipment. At the same time, the government encouraged increased savings to help finance its investment needs. Year after year, Korea ran large trade deficits, especially after the 1979 oil price hike. But it continued to invest more than 30 percent of output per year in addition to its capital stock, making Korea's workers more productive, lowering costs, and improving the quality of exports. Finally, in 1986, Korea's growing exports passed her imports, producing a $4 billion trade surplus, which grew to $8 billion the following year.

These surpluses have allowed Korea to stop borrowing and to begin to repay its debt. From a peak of $47 billion at the end of 1985, Korea now owes only $31 billion. And Korean businesses are now starting to invest abroad. Assuming they continue to pay their debts at current rates, Korea will be a net creditor by 1991!

Korea's success is certainly a credit to its hard-working people, but also to sound government policies and an ample supply of foreign capital. Although Koreans saved 21 percent of their incomes during the 1960s, investment spending ran more than 30 percent of the economy, so outside money was needed to make up the difference. Initial investments in low-technology areas, such as textiles and footwear, paid off big. Textiles and apparel are still Korea's largest export, and Korea is the world's third largest shoe producer. But it has also moved up the value-added chain by making investments in chemicals and steel, then automobiles and electronics.

Korea's success would not have been possible without foreign equipment. Each year, 15 percent of Korea's imports have been spent on capital equipment from all over the world. Walking through the modern factories of Samsung, Hyundai, or Lucky-Goldstar is like a trip to the United Nations, with Korean workers using the latest in American, Japanese, German, and British equipment to produce goods. And the payoffs have been phenomenal, including economic growth rates of more than 10 percent, productivity growth of 11 percent, 3 percent inflation, a 3.3 percent unemployment rate, and a 36 percent savings rate.

U.S. International Debts

In 1888, the United States was the world's largest debtor nation. Just like present-day Korea, we had borrowed the money to finance America's first industrial revolution during the 1800s. Today, at least according to the official numbers, we are once again the world's biggest debtor. This is a somewhat different situation from the Japanese and Korean stories discussed above, many would argue, because the United States is now a mature economy, not a newly developing one, and mature economies are usually providers of capital, not borrowers. It is also disconcerting for the United States to be such a large borrower after having been the world's largest creditor for most of the

past forty years. In fact, as recently as 1982 the United
States was still the world's largest creditor. At that time,
America had outstanding loans and investments in other
countries of $150 billion in excess of its borrowings. But
since 1982, things have changed dramatically. First, foreign investments in the United States accelerated to
record levels. Second, after the run on Continental Illinois
Bank during the summer of 1982, the problems banks
experienced collecting interest on their South American
loans, and the dramatic rise in bank failures in recent
years, U.S. banks drastically pulled in their horns on
extending new loans to foreign borrowers, and U.S. foreign
investment slowed to a trickle. As chart 4.1 shows, America now owes the rest of the world $350 billion, at book
value (which measures the values of assets and liabilities
at historical cost after depreciation, without taking
changes in market prices into account) over and above the
money other countries owe us.

While the United States has been accumulating this
mountain of debt and running increasingly large trade

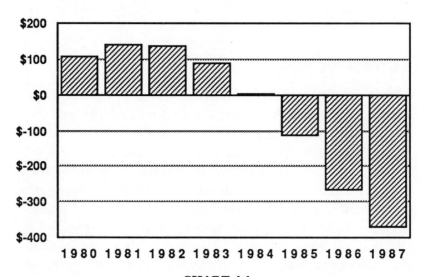

CHART 4.1
U.S. Net Foreign Investments (in billions)

deficits, Japan has been moving in exactly the opposite direction. Japan is now the world's largest creditor and is running huge trade surpluses, by historical standards, in order to offset the large capital outflow. Not surprisingly, since Japan became a large international investor in 1981, the United States has received the lion's share (some 35 percent) of Japanese investments, and Japanese companies have been large buyers of U.S. government bonds. Increasingly, Japanese capital is finding its way into the stock market and into direct investments in the United States, as major Japanese companies set up shop here or buy existing American companies and real estate. Out of the nearly $60 billion of direct investment into the United States in 1987, nearly half came from Japan.

This striking mirror-image nature of the international trade patterns of the United States and Japan, as illustrated in chart 4.2, has made many economists and politicians argue that the Japanese gain is our loss, that having a trade deficit is inherently bad, and that having a trade surplus is inherently good. David Hale summarized

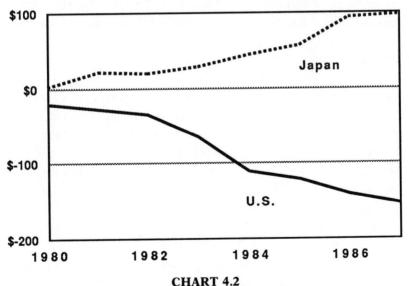

CHART 4.2
Foreign Trade Positions (in billions)

this view in a recent article in the *New York Times:* "America and Japan now have balance-of-payments profiles that are virtually mirror images, with the U.S. the biggest borrower and Japan the largest creditor ... the current global expansion [is] a mixture of Anglo-Saxon hedonism and Oriental thrift." This view is widely accepted among members of Congress, who want to "do something" to bring about balanced trade. Representative John Bryant, (D) Texas, for example, complained: "America has been selling off the family jewels to pay for a night on the town." It sounds downright sinful, doesn't it? But such pat opinions are usually held by people who haven't spent much time looking into what is really behind America's trade deficit and how the foreign capital is being used.

Don't Blame Government Deficits

Because the federal deficit ballooned from $60 billion in 1980 to $237 billion at its peak in 1986—during the same period when the trade deficit got so much larger—some economists began arguing that the trade deficit was *caused* by the rising federal deficit. There is some sense in this reasoning, since budget deficits use capital and trade deficits provide it, but the link is not nearly as clear as most economists would have us believe. Most important, there is no clear link between the two deficits discernible in the data from one year to the next. In 1987, for example, the trade deficit *rose* by $13 billion, even though the federal deficit *fell* by $70 billion. This discrepancy can be explained by remembering that the simple-minded "twin deficits" logic looks only at changes in the borrowing needs of one sector of the economy, the federal government, while foreign borrowings are the result of changes in government, corporate, and personal spending and saving behavior. This is not to say that the federal deficits don't matter—it is only to say that they are not always the biggest game in town. As it happens, in 1987 private savings plunged, even as federal deficits were falling, so on balance we still had to import money from abroad.

Corporate borrowing has also added to the burden of the financial markets. In fact, corporate borrowing has grown by more than government borrowing during the 1980s. From 1980 to 1984, while the net capital coming into the United States amounted to $105 billion, federal, state, and local governments ran a cumulative deficit of $92.1 billion, and business investment spending rose by more than $126 billion.

Others Blame the Consumer

While some blame the Federal deficit, others blame the consumer. Like the good congressman quoted above, many people believe our trade deficit is caused by a mob of unruly consumers out to have a night on the town, with insatiable appetites for foreign-made cars and video recorders. But the breakdown of the trade deficit in chart 4.3

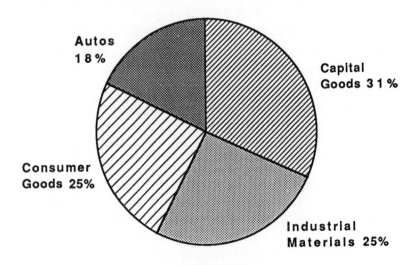

CHART 4.3
Components of U.S. Trade Deficit (1980–1987)

shows that increased imports of consumer goods account
for less than half of the swing in America's trade account
from a balanced position in 1980 to a $171 billion deficit in
1987. In fact, the largest single component of the worsen-
ing trade balance (31 percent) was due to increased
imports of *capital equipment;* the second largest piece was
industrial supplies and *materials* (25 percent)—hardly signs
of runaway consumer spending. Consumer goods (25 percent) and autos (18 percent) filled out the rest of the trade
account. More recent data point even more clearly to the
increasingly important role of capital goods rather than
consumer goods in the trade deficit.

America's Foreign Borrowings Are Paying Off

Most important, America's foreign borrowings are paying
off. The visible results of eight years of foreign
borrowing—international indebtedness, growing interest
payments to service that debt, and an increasing number
of foreign-owned factories, buildings, and companies—
are easy to sensationalize in newspaper and magazine
headlines. But the purpose of international borrowing
is to increase our capital stock so that output, employment, and productivity can expand. And these machines
and equipment are being employed by American
businesses to raise the efficiency and productivity of
American workers. While this makes less exciting
headlines, it is the real story on the effects of foreign
money in America.

Though the economy has been expanding since the
first quarter of 1983, the recovery from the 1982 recession
was led by increased demand for consumer goods and
services and by booming financial markets due to a
tremendous drop in the inflation rate. But personal consumption spending started slowing in late 1986. And by
1987 the recovery switched horses, from consumer goods

and services to capital goods and exports. After a brief dip in the early part of 1987, capital investment began a sustained rise. Beginning in 1987 and continuing into 1988, the growth in both output and employment from manufacturing companies exceeded the growth in the service sector for the first time in eleven years. During this second phase of the expansion, the heavy-metal sectors performed best in terms of growth and profitability. Steel, chemicals, paper companies, and capital equipment producers have been booming, much to the surprise of those who had pronounced America's manufacturing economy prematurely dead in the mid-1980s. The export sector has been booming as well, partly due to the substantial reduction of the dollar since 1985, and partly due to the improved productivity and increased competitiveness of American industry.

The Economy Is a Job-Creating Machine

Since 1980, the American economy has been an unstoppable job machine, spinning out more than 15 million new jobs. In April 1988, the unemployment rate hit 5.4 percent, the lowest in fourteen years, and more Americans were working than ever before in our history, and a higher percentage of Americans had jobs than in any industrial country in the world, including Japan. These new jobs are not all low-skilled, low-paying McJobs either, as some would lead you to believe. Of those 15 million new jobs, 14.5 million were in the service industries, but many of these were in the lucrative financial service sector. And beginning in 1987, the number of manufacturing jobs began to grow faster than the number of service jobs. Even with the substantial decline in financial service jobs that followed the stock market crash of October 1987, the economy continued to create new jobs. Most of these new jobs are directly or indirectly the result of the recapitalization of America.

Higher Productivity at Last

For twenty-three years, from 1960 to 1982, the growth of American productivity sagged sadly behind that of other industrial countries. At its worst, America ranked twelfth among major countries in 1982. Not surprisingly, lack of investment in new tools and machinery, along with sagging output, were the culprits behind this dismal showing of American productivity growth. Since 1982, the situation has reversed dramatically. The combination of robust growth in output and rising investment has boosted American manufacturing productivity growth to nearly double the 1960 to 1982 rate. U.S. manufacturing productivity growth has exceeded Germany's in seven of the past eight years, and Japan's in four of the past six years.

Rising productivity among U.S. manufacturing companies has combined with moderate wage gains to make America a preferred location again for producing a host of industrial products, including automobiles, televisions, and steel. While productivity has been rising, wage increases have been relatively low so labor costs per unit of product have actually *fallen* since 1982. This has put American managers in the enviable position of being able to lower prices and raise profits at the same time.

Not wanting to miss out on a good thing, foreign producers have increasingly been willing to set up shop in the United States to take advantage of our low wage costs and productive workers. Foreign labor is no longer cheap. Partly owing to the declining value of the dollar, and partly due to improvements in U.S. businesses, wage costs in the United States are now virtually equal to Japanese levels and are only two-thirds as high as in German industry, as shown in chart 4.4. Even Taiwanese producers have set up textile and shoe production facilities in the United States because they believe the overall cost of

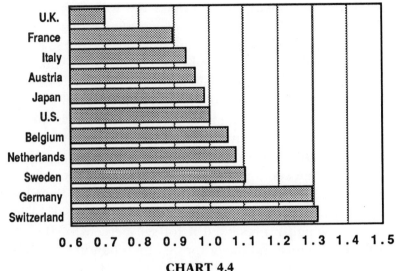

CHART 4.4

Labor Cost Comparisons (U.S. = 1.0)

producing and distributing to the American market is cheaper for goods made here than in Taiwan!

Investment Is the Father of Growth

Necessity may be the mother of invention, but capital accumulation is the father of economic growth. And in the 1980s, a great deal of the capital we have acquired to rebuild our manufacturing sector was brought into the country by foreign investors, including over $37 billion in direct investments by the Japanese. Some industries, such as automobiles, electronics, and textiles, where foreign firms have set up shop and brought new machinery in with them, have benefited directly from inflows of foreign capital by raising productivity and output and lowering costs. Other industries have benefited from the inflow of foreign capital indirectly. Because capital from abroad has helped keep U.S. interest rates low, it has supported

corporate investment, even though the money has gone
primarily into government, not corporate, securities.

During the five-year period from 1980 to 1984, demand for capital goods in the United States grew substantially faster than in Japan. Since the first quarter of 1987,
increases in U.S. capital spending have outpaced growth
in consumer spending. Much of this capital is being
imported. In the first quarter of 1988, for example, U.S.
imports of Japanese capital equipment rose by almost a
third from the same period the year before. In contrast,
imports of consumer goods were up only one-tenth as
much. In 1987 as a whole, capital goods imports rose by
one-fifth, which represented a full 90 percent of the increase in the total inflow of foreign merchandise into the
United States. This imported capital, which worsens our
present trade balance and requires increased foreign debt
in the short term, will nevertheless raise the output and
productivity of American factories and businesses far into
the future.

Export Growth: The Ultimate Source of Repayment

The answer to balancing trade lies in producing more, not
in consuming less. The case histories of countries that
have used foreign debt profitably is that a sudden boom in
exports, not a reduction in imports, has turned around
their fortunes. In fact, imports often rise even more rapidly
than before if commodities or components needed in the
production process come from abroad.

U.S. exports are booming. In 1987, exports grew at a
30 percent pace over 1986, compared to just over 3 percent
growth for the economy as a whole. Gains in export sales
have been shared quite evenly across capital goods, consumer goods, autos, and other products. Agricultural exports have grown, too, although at a slower pace. Some
U.S. exports, such as paper and chemicals, have been

restrained by capacity limitations. As more investment is put in place in the coming years, thereby raising capacity, more products will be available for export and to replace imports. That is how we will eventually reverse the trade deficit.

Many people are not happy to see foreign capital being brought to our shores. Some are worried that we will be the victims of a silent financial invasion, as foreigners take over the political, as well as economic, power in this country. But scare stories that we are selling the country cheaply to foreigners are unwarranted. According to a recent article by Rudiger Dornbusch, professor of economics at MIT, even after the trade deficits of the 1980s foreigners own only 1.65 percent of the tangible assets in America. Yet foreign-owned businesses have created more than 3 million jobs. There is no real economic difference between an automobile produced by Chrysler in Detroit and one produced by Honda in Ohio so far as the impact on the trade account, national output, income, or employment are concerned. In fact, Honda of America was single-handedly responsible for doubling auto exports from the United States to Japan in 1988 over 1987. In 1987, American automakers sold approximately 3,000 cars in Japan, complaining that a negative attitude on the part of consumers toward American products prevented them from substantially increasing this amount. Honda proved this wrong by producing the Accord Coupe in its Ohio plant for export back to Japan. In their first month of sales, April 1988, they sold 2,600 cars and received total orders for 4,000. By the end of the year they expect to sell 5,000 of the model made in America if production in Ohio can keep up. As it turns out, the made-in-America left-hand-drive Accord carries a specialty appeal that is much sought after in status-conscious Japan.

Some argue that goods produced here by foreign-owned plants may help the trade balance now, but they will hurt the current account later when profits are remitted abroad. Working against this fear is the fact that the Japanese have one of the highest reinvestment rates in the world. They are not here to turn a quick buck and cash in their chips. They are here to become major players in our markets over the long haul. Although special interest groups lobby in Washington against the "threat" of increased foreign ownership, state and local governments see the benefits of new businesses. They see the interests of their constituents in terms of jobs and income, not as national labels. Michigan Governor James J. Blanchard, for example, said, "I'm interested in jobs here, first and foremost, and only secondarily in who provides them." Almost every state in the Union, as well as many localities, sends delegations abroad to woo foreign investors to set up shop in their areas.

Beware of What You Want ... You Might Get It

Japan and other countries have loudly demanded that the United States reduce its trade and budget deficits in order to set its house in order and reduce international financial market instability. Of course, for the United States to reduce its trade deficit other countries must reduce their trade surpluses. Japan is already in the process of boosting its imports, producing more abroad and targeting more output to the domestic market in order to reduce exports. And it's working. In fiscal 1987, their trade balance in dollar terms declined by $10 billion on the heels of a 29 percent rise in imports against only a 10.6 percent rise in exports. Taiwan and Korea, which ran large surpluses with the United States in 1987, are under pressure to increase their imports and reduce exports. Both are moving slowly in the same direction as Japan by putting up production facilities in the United States, revaluing their currencies vis-à-vis the dollar, and allowing more imports of U.S. products.

So America's acute shortage of productive capital has turned us into a developing country again. And trade imbalance in the 1980s does not mean the sky is falling; it means that we are reindustrializing our economy, much as we did at the end of the nineteenth century. The trade deficit is a necessary by-product of this redevelopment process. Politics pose the greatest risk to this natural process of rebuilding and repayment. If the adjustment mechanisms that are now working in both the United States and Japan are left to continue on their present courses, the large imbalances of both countries will gradually be reduced and may even be reversed in the next decade. Legislation that stops this healing process artificially, through trade restrictions or capital controls, would leave the United States economy sadly stuck halfway through the adjustment.

5

The Setting Sun: Japan in the Twenty-first Century

I T IS IMPOSSIBLE TO CONSIDER the revitalization of the American economy without examining the prospects for Japan. These two economies, now the first and second largest in the free world, have become increasingly linked to one another since the end of World War II, and the pace at which this interdependence is growing is accelerating as world markets for goods and money are deregulated. This reliance has become a two-way street only in the last decade. The United States helped to finance Japan's postwar reconstruction and has been the largest market for her goods ever since. The rising U.S. trade deficit of the last seven years has been accompanied by Japan's growing surplus, and the loss of market share American manufacturers have suffered at home and abroad has been largely at the hands of their Japanese counterparts. Japan is now the largest market for U.S. securities and is becoming the largest foreign source of investment in U.S. real estate and factories. Given this tight connection, a change in America's fortunes implies a change in Japan's circumstances as well. In fact, changes that are already taking shape in

Japan will help to bring about the recapitalization of American industry and the restoration of our role as an internationally competitive provider of goods.

The Japanese economy has been almost totally restructured during the past forty years. The days when "made in Japan" meant cheaply produced, throw-away party favors are faded memories now that they produce some of the best-quality consumer and high-technology goods available in the world. The efficiency and productivity of Japanese industry have created the largest trade surplus and the highest per-capita income in the world. Because of Japan's industrial strength, it is now a dominant player in world financial markets as well. Within the past ten years, and especially in the last five years, their labors have borne fruit. Japanese producers now control almost a third of the world automobile market and comparable shares of most consumer electronics products. Their financial clout is also preeminent; the Tokyo stock market is now the largest in the world, and Japanese investors hold nearly 10 percent of the outstanding U.S. government debt; seven of the ten largest banks in the world are Japanese.

These developments have spawned the notion in America and Japan that Japanese industry is invincible, and that American financial markets will remain dependent upon its support to keep afloat. Various theories regarding cultural and managerial differences have been put forth to explain or justify these views. The racial homogeneity of the population, the cooperation among government, industry, and labor, lifetime employment, the innate thriftiness and selflessness of the people, and other similar concepts are cited as factors that account for Japan's competitive prowess. Since these factors are unlikely to be duplicated in the United States, these lines of logic have led to the conclusion that the United States will never again rival Japan as a competitive industrial force.

There is something logically inconsistent about crediting innate cultural and political characteristics of a country with what has been a fairly temporary and recent surge to prominence. After all, Japan has run a consistent trade surplus only since 1980, and William Ouchi's book *Theory Z*, which extolls Japanese management, was only written in 1982. If immutable cultural differences were really the cause of Japan's rise and America's downfall, it should have occurred long ago. It seems more reasonable to look to recent phenomena to explain the current differences between the two countries' levels of performance.

Of course we prefer to focus on the sources and uses of capital as the means to industrial strength. This is as true among countries as it is among companies. Those that have ample capital and use it wisely come out ahead. Because the accumulation and deployment of capital in a country are influenced by demographic factors and government policies that change over time, the advantage among countries shifts as well. The rise of Japan's economy can be explained most accurately by their particular demographic structure and government policies, which have encouraged the development of productive capital in the form of factories and machines, while American policies and its population structure have encouraged the destruction of our capital base. But upcoming changes in the age structure of the Japanese population and in certain policy directions in Japan will start to chop away at their desire and ability to invest so much in their own industry, much less to provide large sums of capital to the United States and other developing countries.

These changes will occur over the next two to three decades. The results will not be immediate, but the trends have already been established, trends that are turning Japan into a more consumption-driven economy where less is saved and invested and more is spent and consumed. The success of Japanese industry is now creating an incipient materialism on the part of the people who worked so long and hard for that success, and even more so among their children. Other changes, such as the evolving role of women in the work force, shorter working days and weeks, and a rapidly aging population are beginning to make the Japanese economy look more like America's at a time when Americans are aspiring to duplicate the thriftiness and productivity of the Japanese. These transformations on both sides of the Pacific will contribute to the reemergence of American economic leadership in the twenty-first century.

How Japan Got Where It Is Today

Japan has a population half as large as the United States— 121 million people compared to our 240 million—and they produce just about half as much total output per year as measured by their gross national product of $2 trillion compared to $4 trillion for the United States. Yet in many other significant respects, Japan is now the dominant free world economy, having replaced the United States for the honor during the past couple of years. For example, over the last two years Japan has run the world's largest trade surpluses, equaling $90 billion in their fiscal 1986, which runs April through March, and $76 billion in fiscal 1987. Because they have been selling more than they have been buying abroad, they have been accumulating vast sums of money each year. Some of this money stays with the government in the form of international reserves, now totaling $80 billion, the highest in the world. Some of the money finds its way into the Tokyo stock market, which is now the largest in the world with a total capitalization of $3.5 trillion, compared to $2.3 trillion for the New York Stock Exchange. Not too surprisingly, the Tokyo market was the first to recover totally from the October 1987 crash. The Nikkei Dow returned to a level of 27,000 in April 1988, just six months after the fall. The rest of the money amassed through large trade surpluses is recycled by being invested abroad. Japan is now the largest creditor nation in the world, and it receives more investment income from abroad than does any other country, honors that were held by the United States up until 1985 and 1987, respectively. At the end of 1987 Japan had an estimated $1,090 billion in assets held abroad, with an offsetting $860 billion in liabilities, for a net external position of $230 billion. Japanese interests purchased some $133 billion in assets abroad in 1987, of which nearly $90 billion was in foreign securities and $20 billion was direct investment, such as factories or distributors. The Japanese government has now surpassed the American government as the largest provider of foreign aid and development assistance as well.

All this money gives the Japanese financial clout. The largest securities houses in the world are now Japanese. Nomura, Yaimaichi, Daiwa, and Nikko have replaced the giant financial houses of Merrill Lynch and Salomon Brothers as the biggest hitters in the markets. In credit markets as well the Japanese banks rule the roost. And seven of the top ten were American in 1985. This means that the Japanese can control to a greater and greater extent which countries and companies worldwide can borrow money and how much.

This financial success is the result of Japan's industrial success. When a country earns more than it spends, it accumulates money, just as is the case for a company or family. Japan's high earnings are the result of the highest rate of productivity growth per worker and, therefore, of total output of any major industrial country since the war. Since wages increased by less than output-per-man-hour grew, Japanese industry became more and more competitive as time went by.

The primary reason behind this tremendous expansion of output and productivity in Japan is the fact that their industry has consistently invested large sums in new plant and equipment and tools for the workers. In the forty years since the war, 26 percent of Japan's total annual expenditure has gone toward investment, compared to 14 percent and 16 percent for the United States and Germany. Even today, this high level of investment continues. This rapid rate of capital formation was to be expected after the war. At that time Japan didn't have much modern machinery other than that which had been used to produce war materials. But postwar reconstruction was only the beginning of Japan's industrial miracle. Up until the mid-1960s they were still producing low-quality, cheap products and running large trade deficits. Commentators at the time were concerned that Japan would never be able to produce goods of sufficient quality in large enough quantities to turn their trade deficit to surplus. But Japan continued to build capital machinery and to change the mix of goods it produced. They jumped from producing trinkets to televisions to automobiles almost decade by decade by plowing the experience and profits earned on the simpler products into making more expensive and complicated goods. This rapid transformation was possible because of the continual investment in the new plants and equipment that were needed to produce the next generation of products higher up the value chain.

Certainly, the incredible work ethic of the Japanese plays a part in their success as well. The average "unofficial" work week is fifty-five hours and even today most people have to be forced to take their ten days of paid vacation each year. The lack of labor unrest and days lost to strikes keeps the production lines rolling and helps keep costs down. Quality circles, just-in-time delivery systems, and the like are all contributors to Japan's industrial success, too. But these factors alone cannot explain the continually rapid rate of growth of the economy and of output per worker. No matter how tight your inventory control measures are, once you have just-in-time delivery it does not continue to add to your efficiency. The lack of time off and strike time is the same. These favorable conditions put your output potential a level or two above the country that has less labor cooperation, but they do not continue to boost your output year after year. For that to be the case, workers would have to take fewer and fewer days off each year. That is not the case, even in Japan.

So we come back to the underlying cause of the rapid growth and development of the Japanese economy—continually high rates of capital spending. The results of this sustained high rate of investment are staggering. At last count, Japan had 93,000 industrial robots in operation, compared to 20,000 in the United States and 9,000 in Germany. In terms of total equipment and machinery, Japanese manufacturing workers have twice as much at their disposal as do American workers. During the period 1973 through 1979, Japan increased the amount of capital available for each worker by more than 6 percent per year, compared to less than 1 percent per year in the United States. Faced with these odds, it is little wonder that American products are not price competitive with Japanese goods and that U.S. companies are losing market share. This is not to say that capital is the sole secret of success. Indeed, capital can be squandered just like any other resource. But it is a big and necessary part of the secret.

Saving Pays the Piper

Saying that a country needs a lot of capital in order to be productive and competitive is like saying the way to get rich is to first have a million dollars; it is true but not easy to do. The trick is in getting the money to finance the purchase of all the capital. After that, it is much easier to compete. Japan got the money to invest in the capital equipment that made them competitive primarily through high domestic savings. True, early on they borrowed substantially. But the extraordinary levels of capital spending, running at about a quarter of national income in the early 1970s, as shown in chart 5.1, were largely financed by domestic saving. Since the end of the war, the savings rate in Japan has become a legend, far above that in the United States and most other major countries. Now, even the thrifty Japanese are learning to spend money. After reaching as much as 30 percent of after-tax income, the Japanese savings rate is now running at "only" 16 percent. By comparison, the U.S. savings rate, normally 6 to 8 percent of our incomes, has fallen sharply in the last decade to average less than 3 percent in late 1987.

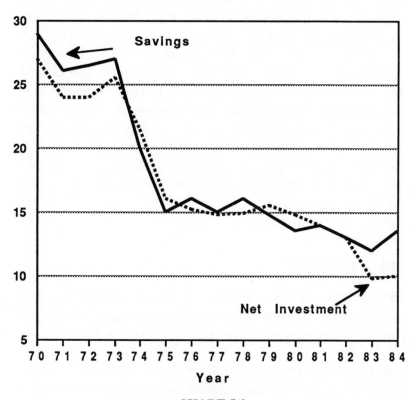

CHART 5.1

Japanese Savings and Net Investment (%)

So the real source of Japan's industrial success has been its high savings rate. This is what allowed Japanese industry to invest in more and more modern equipment every year, allowing the growth of Japanese output to outstrip that of its competitors. This is what raised the output of manufacturing workers every year, and thus kept the prices of products down. This is what has allowed them to accumulate massive financial wealth through huge trade surpluses to the extent that they now dominate the world's financial markets. So the interesting issue now is what motivates the Japanese to save so much? Is it really just in their blood, or is it a cultivated and learned trait?

Demographics Favored Savings

Japan did not have a prolonged Baby Boom following World War II. They experienced a short, sharp rise in the number of babies born for a three-year period, from 1947 to 1949. During those three years, 7 million babies were born. Afterward, the birth rate fell back to more normal levels.

This produced a population structure in Japan that is quite different from that in the United States for the postwar period. Before the war Japan had a pyramid-shaped population structure, with most of the Japanese population concentrated in the zero to forty age categories, and very few people over the age of sixty. After 1949, the high Japanese birth rate leveled off, producing approximately the same number of babies each year for the next forty years. So throughout the postwar period, Japan has had relatively fewer retired people to support, compared to the work force, than have other industrial countries. Also, there was no single age group that was so numerous as to take on the cultural or economic significance of the American Baby Boomers.

Japan, then, has a large group of people now in the forty to sixty age category, meaning they have been in their prime earning and saving age for the past twenty years. The life-cycle theory discussed in chapter 3 suggests that people tend to have the highest savings rates during these ages. Although many cultural differences indicate that the Japanese may have higher savings rates than Americans at all ages, it is also probably true that they are able to put more away during the time that their earnings are peaking and their children have finished school and are supporting themselves.

Those persons born in Japan between the two world wars and immediately after World War II were also influenced to save, perhaps more than their forefathers had been and probably more than their children are being taught today. As a result of the war, the Japanese economy was devastated and much national and personal wealth was lost. Families who sought to restore their wealth had little alternative but to save a large percentage of their earnings in order to accumulate assets, which would support them in their old age and could be handed down to their children.

Also, from a national standpoint, savings were encouraged as a source of funding for rebuilding the country after the war. The Shinto and Buddhist religions do not teach the virtue of thrift, as do the Christian religions, particularly the Protestant varieties influenced by John Calvin. But the interwar and postwar Japanese children were taught this virtue in school through the story of Ninomiya Kinjiro, a large landholder who restored the fortunes of his bankrupt family through hard work and skimping. Although the school children sang a song about a fun-loving fellow named Ohara, who was the epitome of laziness and came to a bad end as a result, they were taught that rewards came from being like Ninomiya, not Ohara.[*]

---

[*] George Fields, *Tokyo Business Today*, April 1988.

Government Policies and Financial Practices Helped, Too

The tax system in Japan since the war has favored savings at the personal level. The Maruyu system allowed almost unlimited accumulation of savings, the earnings on which were not taxable. The official system permitted tax-exempt interest income on principal balances of up to 6 million yen ($50,000) for "nonsalaried" persons, and up to 12 million yen ($100,000) for "salaried" persons. But unofficially, people could hold Maruyu accounts at numerous banks without having their total reported anywhere. The impact of this system was tremendous. When it was dismantled in April 1988, the total balances held in these accounts were estimated at something close to 300 trillion yen ($2.5 billion).

Another aspect of the tax code that encouraged savings and investment was the lack of a capital gains tax on stocks. One had to meet certain requirements to avoid taxes on these gains, such as making less than fifty transactions per year. But again, numerous brokers could be used to getting around this rule. The size of the gains taken in any one year were limited, too, but this was easy to comply with by spreading gains and losses across different tax years. Dividend and interest income also received favorable tax treatment. High-income individuals, who faced a top income tax rate of 80 percent, could elect to have dividends taxed at 35 percent. This rate was even lower for persons in lower tax brackets.

The Japanese tax system includes only miserly deductions for interest paid on mortgages or other forms of borrowings. In addition, there were no provisions for accelerated depreciation on rental properties, hotels, and the like. As a result, the tax system encouraged savings and directed them into stocks and bank accounts rather than into nonproductive "shelters."

Other government policies, in addition to the tax code, encouraged the accumulation of large pools of domestically generated capital. The financial markets in Japan have been highly regulated and tightly controlled by the government through both official and unofficial means. Until 1987, the postal savings banks, where most of the Maruyu savings were held, were restricted from investing more than 5 percent of their funds abroad. Banks were similarly restricted in regard to the amount of foreign lending they could undertake. These capital controls effectively bottled up money in the country, making it available to local companies.

Another aspect of the Japanese financial system that made money available to industry was the underdevelopment of the consumer credit market. Individuals do not borrow much money in Japan and do not use much credit. This is largely cultural, but is also partly institutional. Basically, it is looked down upon in Japan to be in debt. It is taken as a sign of personal weakness and as a lack of discipline. Borrowing for consumption, such as through credit cards, just is not done. Even today a few banks offer credit cards but they are used primarily by foreigners and businessmen, not by housewives. Recently, more and more individuals are taking out equity loans on their real estate, which has appreciated so dramatically. But this money seems to be reinvested in the stock market or in other properties, not spent on vacations and fur coats. In addition, the bonus system, whereby many Japanese receive as much as half of their annual pay in a lump sum, alleviated the need to borrow to make major purchases. Household appliances, the down payment for a home, and other durable goods purchases are generally out of one's annual bonus check.

In summary, the structure of the Japanese tax system, the demographic profile of the population, and various government policies, together with some of the cultural aspects of the country have encouraged savings and investment in Japan during the past forty years. The cultural and economic motivations for saving are intertwined in many ways. For example, it is hard to say whether the extremely high rate of postwar savings was more to restore personal wealth or whether it was the result of indoctrination in the schools or even if it was done out of national pride to help rebuild the country, much as war bonds were purchased in the United States during the war. What does seem clear is that it has been a combination of these factors, and not innate tendencies alone, that have produced a high savings rate and a resulting strong capital base in Japan during the past forty years.

Success Has Its Costs

Becoming the richest country in the world in just over forty years is no small accomplishment. But the extent and speed of this success has created substantial domestic and diplomatic problems for Japan. The island country does not have a tradition of industrialization nor of international trade. It has operated as a very closed society and marketplace throughout its history, which is primarily one of feudal agrarianism, unlike any other global powers that have long trading histories and more open-door policies to foreign ideas and peoples. Japan's rapid transition to an industrial base has disrupted the domestic power structure that has been built around the farmer and the protection of domestic interests. Japan's ruling party, the Liberal Democratic Party, draws much of its support from agricultural interests, which limits its flexibility in revising zoning and tax policies to encourage more beneficial uses of land. This has created a situation where land prices are now so high that the average Japanese has no hope of owning a home. The closed nature of the society is being disturbed by the rapid inflow of foreigners brought about by the commercial and financial needs of modern business. Japan's role in the international community is under fire, as well, as more demands are made for it to contribute more to global welfare, development, and defense.

New Developments and Demographic Changes

If you missed the California Gold Rush, the silver boom, or the Roaring Twenties, you can still experience a place where money flows like water. Just go to Tokyo. Twain said of the silver boom, "Haircuts went for $1,000, and we happily paid it knowing we would make it up tomorrow. We thought it would never end." In Japan, haircuts are not yet $1,000, but they are $100, lunch for two can easily cost $200, and a normal dinner for four can be as much as $1,000—without wine! And just like Twain, the participants in Tokyo's booming real estate and stock markets are full of reasons why it will never end. This is typical of a society where a rapid increase in asset values makes people rich overnight. But, nothing goes up forever. Like all such episodes of sudden riches before it, the Japanese boom will eventually end, too.

Walking down the streets of Tokyo today you are much more likely to see the women decked out in expensive Chanel suits than clad in traditional kimonos. And, sure, the best sushi in the world is still available at the neighborhood restaurant. But right next door is likely to be a pizza shop that delivers. The famous shopping district, the Ginza, is mobbed with *shinjunrui,* the young new breed of consumers who are anxious to flex their buying muscles on gourmet bread-making machines, designer washbasins, and German cars. Government policy is being redirected to encourage more consumption, the population structure is shifting toward more concentrations in higher-consumption age categories, and the needs and wants of the people themselves are changing. Japan is still

Japan, and the old attitudes and patterns of behavior are still prevalent. But new standards and habits are developing and being encouraged by a changing population and policy direction.

The population of Japan is aging faster than that of any other industrial country. The people born during the miniboom of 1947 through 1949 will reach retirement age in 2010. By 2020, 23.6 percent of the population will be sixty-five or over, a higher percentage than in any major industrial country today or projected for the next thirty years. By that time, there will be almost equal proportions of people in each age group rather than a strong base of young or middle-aged people supporting the elderly. As a result, the burden on the system of taking care of retired people will reach 50 percent or more of the national income, compared to about 34.6 percent today. Japan will be worse off than most European countries and the United States in terms of public pension burdens.

So the people who have contributed most to Japan's postwar miracle in terms of high savings rates and long work hours will be retiring over the next thirty years. Not only will this create a drain on the retirement system, as they are removed from the work force, it will also change the patterns of consumption and savings in important ways. A higher proportion of older persons means more expenditures on health care and insurance. Tokai Bank estimates that these expenditures will double from 2.5 percent of income today to nearly 5 percent in 2010. Japan's rising national wealth and income mean fewer working hours and more leisure, so accordingly there will be more expenditures on entertainment and leisure activities; the amounts spent on transportation and communication should grow to nearly three times their current levels, and cultural and amusement expenditures will more than double. Taking all of this into account, Tokai Bank estimates that the savings rate of persons aged thirty-five to thirty-nine will decline from 20.3

percent of after-tax income in 1985 to 10.9 percent in 2010.

Middle-aged Japanese are not waiting to retire to reduce their savings rate, either. One of the primary motivating factors behind their high savings rate since the war has been to rebuild personal and family wealth. For many this has come true, particularly in the last couple of years, during which land prices in Tokyo have more than doubled, and the stock market has risen by 105 percent. These gains in the value of their asset holdings, which in most cases are just on paper, have created a new segment of society in Japan dubbed the New Rich or *nyuu ritchi* by George Fields, chairman of ASI Market Research, Inc., Tokyo, a trend-watching service. These new rich, defined as those whose property assets are valued at more than 100 million yen (about $800,000), were estimated to account for 10 percent of the population as of January 1988. They are spending on luxury goods, primarily European cars and designer clothes, as never before. Furthermore, to escape inheritance taxes on their properties, many new rich borrow up to 70 percent of the value of their properties and put the money into businesses or assets such as stocks that do not carry the same tax treatment as real estate. This type of consumer borrowing is also a new phenomenon in Japan.

The rising tide of retirees and the new rich are not the only reasons for the declining savings rate and changing consumption patterns in Japan—not by a long shot. The young consumers entering the market are very different from their parents. They are spending more, saving less, and using much more credit than the previous generation. "These young people don't save. They would like to spend and enjoy the money they get," said Mr. Fumihiko Sato, an executive with a Tokyo department store that caters to the young, in an interview with the *Financial Times*. And why shouldn't they behave differently? Economic conditions are totally different; these young adults are living and working in the richest country in the world, not the war-ravaged developing country their parents inherited.

Today's youth leaving high school or college are virtually guaranteed employment in an economy where only 2.3 percent of all those seeking work do not find it. And although starting salaries do not compare to the huge initial paychecks often reported by New York law firms or brokerage houses, there is very little chance of getting laid off in Japan. The lifetime employment system is still very strong. Furthermore, many young people can anticipate substantial bequests from their parents, whereas their parents had seen their family's wealth destroyed in the war. The most valuable asset held by most middle-aged Japanese today is their home. Even though very few young can now afford to buy a home, well over half of those aged fifty to fifty-four own their own home. More than three-quarters of all extended families, where the parents move in with their children as is still quite common, own the home they live in, and the children can anticipate receiving this home when the parents die. Monetary bequests are substantial as well, since the average savings balance equals one year's salary.

Education influences reflect this new set of circumstances. Rather than quoting stories about Ninomiya, the farmer who saved his family from bankruptcy by saving, schoolchildren and young adults are reading the *Mayekawa Report*. This famous study was presented to the government in 1986 by Haruo Mayekawa, a former governor of the Bank of Japan, as a guideline for adapting to the pressures of Japan's large trade surplus. It encourages Japanese to buy more goods, domestic and imports alike, and urges domestic manufacturers to orient their products and their marketing strategies toward increasing sales at home, rather than abroad.

These changes in attitudes, needs, and influences are

working to increase consumption in Japan dramatically. The most popular products are those that offer something called "plus-alpha," an element of additional perceived value over the functionality of the good. Products that deliver prestige, quality, or emotional appeal command premium prices in Japan's affluent marketplace. Foreign cars have been the most rapidly growing status symbol during the past two years. This boom is spilling over into domestically made car markets as well—especially luxury cars.

The most popular new products, other than automobiles, are those that also offer the "one-level-higher" life-style, as shown in table 1. Products that offer convenience, use high technology, add to one's comforts, or are used in leisure activities are selling like hot cakes. Automatic home bread makers, large-screen televisions, satellite dishes, and compact disc players top the list of recent successes. They also sound suspiciously more like an American Yuppie's shopping catalogue than a mama-san's wish list. Last, but not least, the changing role of women in the workplace and marketplace is a big part of the new affluence. More women are now entering the work force with university degrees, staying longer, working after marriage and motherhood, and moving to higher paying, more senior positions. At present, female workers over the age of thirty-five account for nearly two-thirds of the female work force. Almost the same number are married, and thirty-five percent are university graduates. Products targeted at working women are among the best sellers. Washbasins designed to let you wash your hair in the morning without having to take a shower; Attack brand detergent, which supposedly removes micron-sized dirt particles from clothes; Misty brand cigarettes; and several new women's magazines top the 1987 new product hit list. New boutiques such as The New York are opening up to bring the fashion, ideas, and spirit of the modern work-

TABLE 1   Japan's Hot Products of 1987

"One level higher"	Automatic home bread makers, large screen television sets, new houses, draft beer, "Formula Shell Super X" gasoline
High technology	"Attack" detergent, parabola satellite antennas, four-wheel steering cars, mini-component stereo sets, and compact disc players
Romance	"Sarada kinenbi" (salad day), tanka anthology, Nissan "Be-1" car, membership resort clubs, pets
Strong yen	Overseas trips, imported cars, foreign real estate
Convenience	Microwave ovens, precut vegetables, long-distance telephone calls
Comfort	House renovation, No Time gum (substitute for brushing), air cleaner, germ control socks
Health and sports	Delicious Water, bottled oxygen, bicycles, athletic clubs, health drinks, stress treatments
Fun and games	Cassette-recorded books, billiards, sea cruises
Services	Voice mail, party organizers, caterers, services for Japanese living overseas, personalized import services

Source: Dentsu, Inc.

ing woman to Japan's businesswomen. Middle-aged men in Japan often credit their housewife, or *oku-san*, with the high savings rate of the family. The men claim they hand their paychecks over to their wives and have to ask for their own spending money during the rest of the month. The naturally more conservative nature of these *oku-san* causes them to stash away as much of the family income as possible. As they become less prevalent in Japanese society, and two-earner families become more commonplace, it will show up in the savings rate.

Government Policy Changes

Bob Hope once said, "You know how it makes you feel
when a friend gets ahead. Sick." To some extent the
demands being placed on Japan today by other countries
to reduce its trade surplus and contribute more to international development and defense reflects this type of
sour grapes response. But there are also legitimate reasons
to expect a country that is now the richest in the world to
behave a little bit differently from when it was a developing nation. Since the 1970s international pressures have
been growing to stimulate domestic spending; encourage
and allow more imports; deregulate the participation of
foreign banks, securities houses, and insurance firms in
Japanese markets; and contribute more to area defense
and multinational organizations. That's when it became
obvious that Japan was now one of the big boys, no longer
requiring protection and special status to encourage its
economy. Pressure has intensified during the 1980s as
Japan's trade surplus with the United States and Europe
has ballooned. Japan's trade surplus with the United
States was $7 billion in 1980 and $52 billion in 1987. The
increase with the European Economic Community has not
been quite as dramatic, but the surplus there has doubled.
And during a period when European unemployment rates
have been stuck at about 10 percent, such success by
Japan, with 3 percent unemployment, has not been very
popular.

Partly in response to international pressures, and
partly because of their own recognition that they must
now begin to assume a more mature role internationally,
the Japanese government in 1985 commissioned former
governor of the Bank of Japan Haruo Mayekawa to study
and report on the need for economic restructuring. The
initial *Mayekawa Report* was presented in April 1986.
However, the revised and most well known report was

reissued in May 1987. This hard-hitting report was a real break from traditional Japanese responses to such pressures, which usually claimed that progress was being made and that moving too much faster would be dangerous. In contrast, Mayekawa stated:

> As a country largely dependent upon free trade, a country accounting for one-tenth of world GNP, and the world's largest creditor nation, Japan must take the initiative in rolling back protectionism and defending the free trade system by seeking to achieve an internationally harmonious external balance and to make a positive contribution to the international community.

The report recommended reducing the external trade imbalances as quickly as possible, deregulating domestic markets and improving import access to Japan. Industry was to restructure to provide more to the home market and less for export, direct foreign investment was to be encouraged, and markets were to be opened to foreign providers of services and goods.

Many people said they had heard all this from Japan before, and they would believe it when they saw the results. Well, the results are starting to come in, and this time it looks serious. Starting with the trade sector, rough steps have been taken to start bringing down the huge surpluses. In September 1985, Japan and the other major industrial countries met at the Plaza Hotel in New York and came out with what has been called the "Plaza Accord." This was an agreement to drive down the value of the dollar, which would make foreign goods more expensive in the United States and make American goods more competitive abroad. Since that time, the yen has doubled in value against the dollar. While the U.S. trade balance has been slow to respond to this change, the volume of Japanese imports and exports began turning almost immediately. In 1986 imports rose nearly 20 percent from the previous year, and in 1987 they were up another 10 percent. Among the biggest gainers in 1987 were automobiles, steel, textiles, and lumber. Unfortunately, the United States did not benefit much from many of these items, other than lumber, since the Japanese, like the Americans, seem to turn to European cars and clothes when they look to go up-scale. Overall, Japanese exports, which had been rising by about 7 percent in volume terms, declined by 2 percent in both 1986 and 1987. When looked at from the Japanese perspective, they are shipping fewer goods abroad and buying more foreign-made products.

Restructuring Domestic Industry

These changes in the trade picture are obviously tied to the consumption boom described above. But they are also associated with some major changes in the composition of Japanese manufacturing. For example, steel output has been cut dramatically, requiring the relocation of 40,000 workers, and coal output will be cut in half by 1991. There is now only one aluminum smelting plant in Japan, compared to seven just five years ago. Television production is down 60 percent, radios are down 40 percent, and even automobile production has slipped by 10 percent. But as this restructuring of Japanese manufacturing continues, wages or employment may have to decline.

Part of this restructuring of Japanese industry is being accomplished by Japanese companies setting up more and more production facilities abroad. Automobile and electronic producers, for example, are moving into the United States in order to avoid further trade restrictions and to be closer to their ultimate consumer. Textile, ship, steel, and other producers are transferring their production locations to other, lower cost Asian countries such as Thailand.

This is a positive development for the countries receiving Japanese capital because it channels some of Japan's surplus capital to their shores, adding to their productive potential, output, and employment. For Japan, it means that the rate of capital accumulation is slowing down and that productivity and output cannot be expected to continue rising at their previous breakneck speeds. It would be premature to anticipate a deindustrialization of Japan. But it would be equally myopic to deny that the increasing export of Japan's capital will not reduce the base upon which much of their postwar success has been built.

Spend—It's Good for the Economy

As a complement to changes in international trade policy, the government has made some real revisions in their domestically oriented policies. Consumption has been directly encouraged in several ways. A minor income tax cut in 1987 added about 0.5 percent to personal spendable income. Another more sweeping tax reform, which will reduce personal taxes further, is now being considered, especially for middle-income persons. While some of the reduced revenue will be replaced by the introduction of a new sales tax, which will have the effect of reducing consumption, that will be only a one-time adjustment to the level of spending, but tax incentives to save and invest have been cut and will be cut further. In addition, the Maruyu system of tax-exempt savings was done away with in April 1988. All interest and dividends are now taxable, and the new tax proposal will add a tax on capital gains on securities, something Japan has never had in modern times. Overall, this tax reform will promote more spending and less saving.

The government has also introduced subsidies to the housing industry—more incentive for the Japanese to spend their money. To give further help to the consumer to spend his money, the government is also relaxing long-standing regulations on the locations and hours of shops. Until very recently, large department stores or supermarkets could open up in local communities only with the permission of local merchants, who clearly were not interested in helping the wolf enter the chicken coop. But now the authorities are granting permission for more of the distribution-minded super-stores to open up, despite local opposition. This is bringing longer hours, more selection, and even some price competition to Japanese consumer markets—things that were just about unheard of a few years ago.

The government is doing even more to lead the horse to water by revising work laws to give people more leisure time. Since April 1988, Japanese government workers have been enjoying five-day work weeks every other week, quite a change in a country where working six-day weeks is the norm. And work laws were revised to make the official number of hours in the work week forty-six, instead of the previous forty-eight. Japan's official Economic Planning Agency estimates that a five-day work week would increase consumer spending by about $13 billion per year. Companies are also being asked to encourage their workers to take all of the time off to which they are entitled. At present, most workers use only 55 percent of their paid annual vacation time. This amounts to about ten days off per year, plus holidays, of which, admittedly, there are a large number in Japan. Just revising the Labor Standards Law will not ensure that many more people take more time off in a country where working long hours is still considered a virtue. But, as chart 5.2 shows, the trend toward working less, and taking more leisure time during which you are likely to spend money, is undeniable—and now the government is encouraging it.

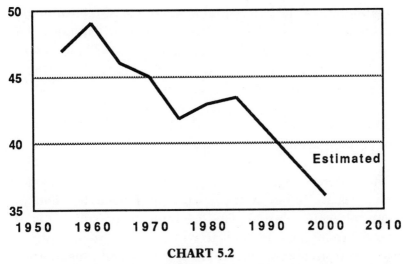

CHART 5.2
Fewer Working Hours in Japan (hours/week)

The Government Is Spending, Too

Finally, government purchases are adding to domestic spending, too. Because corporate profits and personal income have increased by more than expected, and because the government made a windfall profit of nearly $10 billion on the sale of some of its shares in the huge communications giant, NTT, there has been ample spending power in the government, even with tax cuts. In 1987, the government passed a supplementary budget for public works of about $16.6 billion. These are not just road repairs and sewage systems. The extra money is financing large-scale projects such as the Tokyo Bay Bridge and Tunnel and the new Kansai International Airport outside Tokyo—increased expenditures that are expected to be continued for several years.

All of these enhancements to domestic spending have been supported by loose monetary policy, i.e., running the printing press overtime. Keeping plenty of money in the system makes credit available for home purchases, stock purchases, and business expansion. Because inflation has not been a problem, loose money has also helped keep interest rates low for the time being. This also helps to stimulate borrowing and spending.

The Sun Is Not Quite So High in the Sky

These demographic, policy, social, and even cultural changes in Japan will all work to reduce the pace of capital accumulation. The declining trade surplus is already reducing the rate at which Japan is bringing in money from abroad. Increased spending and consumerism will begin to erode the huge domestic pool of savings that has backed massive industrial investment. Changing tax laws and shifting patterns of demand will redirect the remaining pools of funds into different, less productive areas of the economy. The country is being transformed from one in which the rates of savings, investment, productivity growth, and economic expansion are the highest in the industrial world to one that more closely approximates the norm for a mature economy.

As the Japanese economy moves into this more mature stage, it will begin to take on more of the characteristics of its European and American peers. Expenditures for social welfare and international assistance will continue to increase. Larger numbers of people will be employed in the service sector where productivity is harder to boost. Factories will be replaced by hotels and exports by imports. When these trends have proceeded long enough, the trade surplus will turn to deficit and the capital surplus to shortage.

During this transition, however, Japanese capital will be a critical contributor to the reindustrialization of American goods. So the changes that are taking place on both sides of the Pacific are highly complementary. But there is no assurance that they will proceed at the same pace, or that they will balance out year by year. Any major economic transition is accompanied by upheavals in prices and the fortunes of businesses and the markets. When the transition is occurring in the two largest economies in the world, even more disruption and upset can be anticipated.

The risk to the future is not that America will not change, nor that an invincible Japan will block that change, but rather that the change in each is not sufficiently synchronized to be smooth. If the American Baby Boomers do not increase their savings rate soon enough to offset declining inflows of capital from Japan, then U.S. financial markets could be in for rising interest rates and a declining stock market for a period of years. If Japanese consumers do not boost their buying rapidly enough to offset declining exports, the Japanese economy may be in for a period of stagnant growth.

This risk is more in the nature of short-term setbacks that could occur within the transitions outlined above. The trends of change are already set in motion. The process of moving in these directions looks inevitable. The sun, if not yet beginning to set, is rapidly approaching high noon.

6

Pumping Iron:
The Rebirth of the Rust Bowl

L IKE THE NINETY-EIGHT-POUND WEAKLING in the comic book
ad, American manufacturing companies by the late
1980s got tired of getting sand kicked in their faces.
Slowly, one by one, they started pumping iron, retooling
and restructuring their operations to become more competitive.

The first half of this book describes the series of events
that made America lose its competitive edge in manufacturing and identifies the forces that are beginning to turn
that situation around in our favor. This chapter describes
examples of what actual companies are doing to rebuild
their businesses to be more competitive and improve their
returns on capital.

Many companies have already taken the cure by
ridding themselves of the wrong stuff they accumulated
during the 1970s, and by retooling their businesses for
no-frills, hard-nosed competition in the 1980s. Not surprisingly, the most exciting stories come from the industries
that were hit the hardest by the inflation-deflation roller
coaster of the last two decades. Steel, chemical, rubber,

and automobile companies have been pushed to the brink, and many of them have come back tougher, more bottom-line oriented, with smaller, more focused, and more profitable firms. Other companies, such as Coca-Cola, have been driven to manage their assets more wisely, not because they were in trouble but because they realized that it is tougher to stay ahead of the competition in the current environment. Still others, such as General Electric, have stayed out of trouble by ruthlessly cutting costs and scrapping unprofitable businesses before the wolf came knocking, playing the game of musical chairs and winning. Even city governments, such as Detroit and Peoria, capitals of the Rust Bowl in their own right, have taken it upon themselves to turn their fortunes around, actively seeking to bring in new domestic and foreign businesses to provide jobs for their people, restoring their downtown areas, and helping to bring about an industrial renaissance where there once were rusting factories.

The work is going on, but there is still a lot to do. Many cities in the Midwest still suffer from unemployment rates much higher than the national average due to plant closings or major cutbacks at key local employers. And many companies still have a long way to go before they reestablish themselves as viable competitors for the long haul. But the process of rebuilding industrial America is well underway and is gaining speed. The real opportunities for investors are in identifying the companies, industries, and regions that are just beginning to work out their problems but are still unrecognized by the market.

When the Going Gets Tough

Sometimes things have to get bad before they can get better. Nobody likes to make the tough decisions. And no manager likes to tear his company apart and turn it inside out looking for a new formula that will work. But we all make the tough decisions when we have to, when times get tough enough and business gets bad enough to make us face up to reality.

Business conditions were certainly bad enough in 1982. The economy was caught in the middle of the longest and deepest recession since the 1930s. American industry was losing ground abroad and losing market share at home to a rising tide of imports. For over a decade the growth of productivity in manufacturing had been lower in the United States than in any of the other twelve major industrial countries. Despite little productivity growth, wages had risen at nearly 10 percent per year, so costs were rising. Inflation was out of hand, running above 10 percent and cresting at 14 percent in 1980. And the quality of our manufacturing products failed to keep pace with other major producers. By 1982, it seemed that matters could get no worse.

In business it was clear that it was time to get tough or get out. Personal and corporate bankruptcies soared, along with bank failures. Commodity prices tumbled, precious metal prices collapsed, and oil prices fell from nearly $40 per barrel in 1981 to less than $10 per barrel by mid-1986 (good news for consumers and energy-dependent businesses, but devastating for the oil companies and related industries and for the banks that loaned them money). Farmland prices sagged, dragging farm community banks and the Farm Credit System down with them. And the prices of the mining, oil drilling, and farming equipment went down under the auctioneer's gavel. At one point in 1986, there was an auction in Houston where oil rigs were sold for less than it had cost their owners to transport them to the auction site. Needless to say, the next auction was a little short on inventory. Farmers and their bankers suffered the same fate. The price of prime Minnesota farmland fell from a high of $4,000 per acre in 1980 to $750 per acre in 1986. Many farmers found that their best bet was to walk away from the mortgaged land, rather than try to hang on to service the mountainous debts by selling crops at half the price they fetched when the loans were made. This kind of policy made the Bank of America the largest landowner in California, next to the federal government.

The moral of the story is that those who own a depreciating asset aren't the only ones hurt by falling prices. When the prices of durable goods in the resale markets fall—i.e., auctioned drill rigs or farm equipment in the 1980s—firms that produce new durable goods find that they are priced out of the market by their own past output, and their managers, their workers, their bankers, and their shareholders suffer. During the deflation of the 1980s, for example, used cars, not foreign cars, became the greatest source of competition for Detroit, as want ads were filled with items offering to give up recently purchased cars to anyone willing to assume the finance charges. And people decided they would drive their current car a while longer rather than buy a new one, raising the average age of a car on the road by two years from 1980 to 1985, which had the effect of eliminating nearly two years of average new car sales. It was not the Japanese who dealt the most serious blows to the American automakers, it was deflation that made their own used cars come back to haunt them.

By 1983, the drive to cut costs and write down obsolete capacity was in full swing. During the three-year period through 1986, American industry wrote down or sold off more than $1 trillion in assets, and the papers were filled with restructuring stories every day. Many companies sold marginal or unprofitable businesses to raise cash, most for less than book value, so earnings took a heavy hit. Other firms, such as Union Carbide, Exxon, and Bank of America, raised cash by selling their corporate headquarters buildings. As the recession stayed in place, companies looked to cut payroll, too. But this time managers got pink slips along with their production workers.

All told, the Fortune 500 companies reduced their payrolls by more than 1 million people in the early 1980s.

Back to Basics

In the 1960s, many managers believed they could effectively apply the operations, financing, and marketing skills they had learned in one industry to running almost any other business. They believed economies of scale would make larger businesses more efficient. And they believed that a company made up of many different businesses would be less prone to business cycles. So conglomerates grew like mushrooms.

But the harsh economic climate of the 1980s proved to be an unwelcome place for such large, poorly focused businesses. Thus many of the asset sales unleashed during the restructuring binge were made by conglomerates seeking to redefine and refocus their basic businesses. By selling off noncore businesses, management could intensify its efforts to improve the operations of their core businesses.

Mobil Oil is a company whose diversification moves never really panned out. In 1976, they acquired Montgomery Ward, a consumer retail chain. From that day forward, Ward lost money—over $415 million in 1981 and 1982—proving for all time that an oil man should drill holes, not sell washing machines. Finally, in 1985, the management of Mobil decided that too much was enough, and spun Ward off into an independent company, headed by Bernard Brennan, the brother of Edward Brennan, the CEO of Sears, Roebuck and Company. The sale required a write-off of an additional $508 million for Mobil, but it turned out fine for Brennan. He quickly sold Ward's $1.2 billion catalog operation and the sick discount chain, and turned the broad-based retailer into a specialty store that produced six straight quarters of profits through the end of 1987.

There are many other examples of companies getting back to basics. United Technologies folded its semiconductor unit and sold a telecommunications business for a loss of over $400 million in order to focus on its main business of making industrial products. Fairchild Industries, an electronics company, took a $100 million write-off to get out of a commercial aircraft venture in an attempt to return to profitability and pay down its debt. And Goodyear sold its energy and aerospace companies in order to concentrate on making tires at a profit. In every case, the lesson was the same: Stop wasting your time and resources doing things you're not good at, and concentrate your energies on what you do best.

But most of the restructuring and cost cutting in the 1980s was done by companies that had simply let their core businesses get too fat and unprofitable. The irony of the write-offs is that managers often wasted a lot of time agonizing over the cuts they had to make, fearing that their shareholders would lose confidence if they confessed their mistakes. Instead, the companies that took the hard steps early were often rewarded by investors with an increase in their stock prices, and their CEOs were heralded for their toughness and honesty.

Schlumberger, the international oil services company, announced in December 1986, one of the biggest write-offs in corporate history, with a $1.7 billion charge to profits. More than half of this charge resulted from losses on fixed assets, such as drilling and logging equipment. The company, which had earned high praise in the past for its astute management, had fallen prey to the big ideas that accompanied high oil prices and paid too much for the equipment and companies they acquired. Like other oil companies, they had borrowed money to expand, which came back to haunt them when oil prices fell.

As for the oil industry, all of the major companies took write-offs and severely cut their costs in the 1980s. And for good reason. During the days of rising oil prices in the 1970s, the carpets in the executive suites got a little thicker, the prints on the walls were replaced with original oil paintings, and many executives came to believe that their newfound profits were attributable to their personal management skills. And then the bottom dropped out for oil prices. Companies that had made reasonable profits just a decade before, when oil sold for only $2 per barrel, were unable to break even at $20 per barrel!

Exxon was one of the most aggressive at cutting costs and restructuring operations to stay even with falling oil prices. In March 1986, they announced a 30 percent reduction in capital spending and a drastic slowdown in new exploration. Within days they also announced they were eliminating some overseas operations and cutting headquarters staff, on top of the 20 percent world-wide staff cuts they had already made since 1981. They used much of the money they saved to acquire oil reserves from cash-poor companies. ARCO got rid of its credit card operations and lowered prices in an attempt to increase its market share while cutting its administrative costs on credit purchases. Other companies soon followed their lead. Chevron paid over $13 billion for Gulf Oil in 1984, then sold refinery assets and its southeastern service stations to Standard Oil of Ohio. Then, in 1985, they divested 60 percent of Gulf Canada as well. And Getty Oil, one of the grand old names in the business, was sold to Texaco, in one of the most controversial transactions of the decade.

The managers who were tough enough to cut costs and take their write-offs quickly were the lucky ones. Those who were too slow or too timid became targets for takeovers. In a normal year, many mergers and acquisitions take place having nothing to do with bad management; they represent the ordinary changing of dance partners at the end of a song. But when takeovers reach the levels of the 1980s, there is more going on than the normal ebb and flow of business. They are a sign that

entrepreneur investors believe they can run businesses
better than their current managers. Companies that are
poorly focused, that hold excess assets, or that have weak
market positions tend to sell for less than the value of their
combined assets in the stock market, and are sitting ducks
for investors willing to buy fixer uppers and inject the
missing management discipline.

Takeover specialists like Irwin Jacobs—fondly referred to as "Irv the Liquidator"—made millions of dollars
proving that a whole company is often worth less than the
sum of its parts. Jacobs bought whole businesses when
their stock prices were depressed, then sold their component divisions at premium prices. When Jacobs bought
AMF, the sporting goods company that had diluted the
value of a once strong specialty company into oil field
services, motorcycles, and other far-flung interests, he was
able to sell off the noncore businesses for enough money to
pay for the entire acquisition, effectively buying the core
business for nothing! Some companies bought whole businesses just to acquire a particular division that comple-
mented their long-term strategy, then sold off the
remaining pieces to other firms. Wells Fargo, for example,
sold off more than $8 billion of assets after it acquired
Crocker Bank. And Rorer sold two of its divisions to raise
money to pay down a portion of the debt it used to finance
the purchase of Revlon's prescription drug business. Other
companies avoided takeover, but in order to defend themselves against outside buyers ended up making many of
the same changes that would have been made by an
acquirer.

This first stage of restructuring for low inflation,
involving major surgery on overhead, operating costs, and
excess assets, has been going on since 1982. The payoff in
costs and improved productivity have been tremendous.
Since 1982, productivity in American manufacturing has
increased by more than 4 percent each year, compared
with only 1.3 percent per year during the previous decade.

Profits were initially lower due to the massive asset write-offs the manufacturing companies were forced to take to clean up their balance sheets, but they began rising sharply in 1987 as rising revenues and lower costs finally started to pay off. This is just the beginning of a long period of rising profits and growing companies.

Rebuilding American Companies

Now that the write-offs are behind us and the deflation is over, American companies are building for the future. This means investment in new equipment, additional capacity, and new materials-handling and productivity-enhancing systems. The improvements to American manufacturing companies made in the early 1980s have already started to pay off, giving us higher productivity growth than all other major industrial countries except Japan since 1982. And since 1985, as table 2 shows, American industry has

TABLE 2   International Productivity and Cost Comparisons (Annual Percent Changes in Local Currencies)

	1973–1980	1980–1985	1986	1987
Productivity				
United States	1.2	3.7	3.7	3.8
Japan	5.7	5.9	2.8	4.2
Germany	3.2	3.5	1.9	2.5
United Kingdom	0.1	5.7	2.9	—
Labor Costs				
United States	8.5	2.1	− 0.4	− 2.4
Japan	5.8	− 1.1	0.7	− 1.2
Germany	5.4	1.8	3.1	3.5
United Kingdom	18.5	3.3	5.0	—

Source: U.S. Department of Labor, Bundesbank, and Japanese Productivity Institute. Taken from Morgan Stanley, *Economic Perspectives*, December 9, 1987.

even outperformed the Japanese in both productivity and labor costs.

These improvements have not been concentrated in any one industry, but spread evenly across all of manufacturing. As chart 6.1 shows, American productivity gains have exceeded those in Japan from precision instruments and nonelectrical machinery to apparel, rubber, and plastics. These productivity improvements, together with reduced wage costs and the falling dollar, have made America one of the cheapest places in the industrial world to produce manufactured goods.

Some of the most striking improvements have taken place in the most unlikely places. Many analysts, for example, had declared the U.S. steel industry dead after watching it lose more than $12 billion between 1982 and 1986. They claimed that we could never again compete with the cheap labor and modern production systems being used in Korea and Japan. But in 1987, the industry recorded a $1 billion profit, prompting *Business Week* to run a feature called "Cancel the Funeral—Steel Is on the Mend." However, the turnaround was not accomplished overnight, it was the result of major changes made throughout the 1980s. Since 1982, the steel industry reduced its capacity by more than 30 percent, and total employment by nearly half. American steelmakers spent more than $8 billion on new continuous-casting operations and other modern equipment and made great strides in improving both the quality of their product and their delivery systems. There are still risks, of course. A serious economic downturn would throw steel makers back into the red, and both Wheeling-Pittsburgh and LTV are still in Chapter 11. But the strong companies, especially USX and Bethlehem Steel, are making profits and growing.

Bethlehem Steel is a good example of a company whose managers have been doing all the right things, and that is seeing those improvements reflected in a rising stock price. Though Bethlehem's managers have not yet

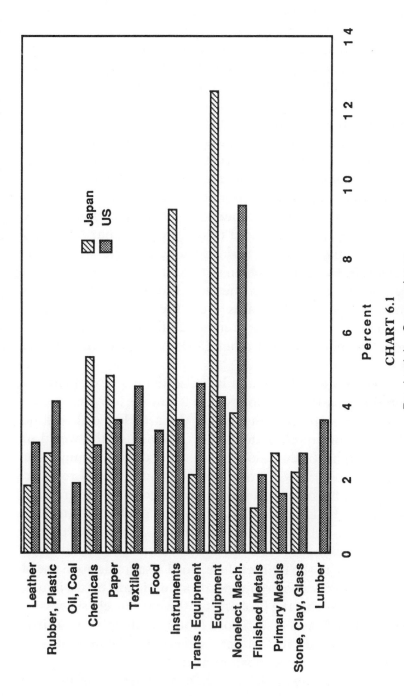

Percent

CHART 6.1

Productivity Comparisons

succeeded in winning the respect and regard of their peers (in a January 1988 *Fortune* survey of executives, directors, and financial analysts, Bethlehem Steel was ranked among the ten least-admired companies), their stock rose in value more than that of any company on the ten most-admired list. *Fortune* asked Walter Williams, Bethlehem's chief executive officer, how he would explain the apparent inconsistency of the survey results. Emphasizing their progress in cutting costs and raising productivity (Bethlehem's $2 billion in new investments allowed them to reduce the cost of producing a ton of steel by 25 percent), Williams explained that other executives simply had not yet been educated to the progress that American steel companies were making in rebuilding their businesses. But with Bethlehem's stock price up more than 160 percent in a year when the Dow Industrials rose by less than 1 percent, Williams won the survey that really counted, that of his shareholders. In the final analysis, it is your shareholders, not other CEOs, who pay your annual bonus.

Ford Motor Company has also done an excellent job rebuilding a tired company into a star performer. From a mediocre position at the turn of the decade, Ford became the most profitable automobile company in the world in 1987. Eight billion dollars in new capital equipment during the 1980s improved product quality and reduced the critical time period it required to go from the drawing board to the assembly line on new models. Design decisions were returned to the engineers, who introduced a new, aerodynamic look to Ford's cars that found good acceptance in the marketplace. Ford also made good use of their minority ownership position in Mazda by designing a new sports car, the Probe, after the immensely successful Mazda RX-7. As a result, Ford Motor, with only two-thirds the sales of General Motors, exceeded GM in profits in 1986 and 1987 by a substantial margin.

Some companies have had sufficient courage and

foresight to make the changes they needed to make without getting in trouble. These are the companies that have been consistently well-managed over the years, companies who know how to manage their capital resources. They didn't have perfect foresight that allowed them to avoid making mistakes—nobody does. But they had the courage and judgment to identify their mistakes early and remove them before they got too expensive.

One of the best such examples is General Electric. Founded by Thomas Edison in 1878, GE is the only surviving charter member of the original (1896) Dow Jones Industrial Average. The carpets are so thick in GE's executive offices, the story goes, not for luxury but so you can't hear the footsteps of the guy walking behind you ready to take your job if you trip up. GE is ruthlessly demanding of its managers, especially those who are charged with bottom-line responsibility for its business units. They know why they are at GE—to deliver steady high returns to their shareholders—and somehow, through all the decades since GE's founding, the commitment of its managers has grown stronger, not weaker.

GE's current CEO, Jack Welch, has decentralized the company, and pushed more decisions down to the operating people than had been the case with his predecessor, Reginald Jones. And GE has been extremely aggressive at restructuring for low inflation and tax reform in the 1980s. Since Welch took over in 1981, GE has cut 25 percent of its work force—more than 100,000 people. During this same period revenues rose by 48 percent, giving GE a staggering 98 percent increase in revenues per employee. In the 1980s, GE also sold its mining business, Utah International, when it became clear that disinflation had undermined the profitability of commodity businesses and sold its small appliance business to Black and Decker. Then GE acquired Kidder, Peabody, the investment bank, and RCA, whose assets included the television network NBC. GE is obviously a much different company today than it was when Jack Welch took over at the beginning of the 1980s. The commitment of her managers to doing whatever is necessary to earn top dollar for GE shareholders puts General Electric virtually in a class by itself as a well-run giant company.

Foreign Companies Are Investing in America, Too

Foreign companies are setting up shop in the United States in record numbers, bringing with them new capital equipment and management skills that are giving our industrial base a tremendous shot in the arm. Many of these foreign firms are making major long-term commitments to their American operations by bringing in boatloads of new capital equipment, taking over facilities abandoned by American firms, and producing jobs and quality products for sale here and abroad. This foreign capital has played an increasingly important role in the revitalization of American industry during the 1980s, and accounts for an important part of the productivity gains we described above.

Japanese automakers are the most prominent foreign companies now operating in the United States. Honda's operation in Marysville, Ohio; Nissan's plant in Smyrna, Tennessee; Toyota's Georgetown, Kentucky, factory; and other Japanese operations located in the United States will produce nearly 2 million cars in 1989, as shown in table 3, about as many cars as we imported from Japan in 1987. These cars wear Japanese logos, but they are American products, using American steel, American workers, and American sales and service operations. These plants play just as important a role in rebuilding American industry and the parts of the country where they are located as GM, Ford, or Chrysler plants do for their communities.

TABLE 3   Japanese Auto Production in the United States

Company	Year	Investment (millions)	Capacity (Number of Units)	Total Capacity
Honda	1982	$530	360,000	360,000
Nissan	1983	$745	240,000	600,000
Toyota/GM	1984	$500	250,000	850,000
Mazda	1987	$800	300,000	1,150,000
Toyota	1988	$800	200,000	1,350,000
Mitsubishi/ Chrysler	1988	$600	240,000	1,590,000
Fuji/Isuzu	1989	$500	240,000	1,830,000

Source: Japan Economic Journal

Now that the Japanese automakers are firmly rooted on our shores, their traditional parts suppliers are following in large numbers. The largest of these is Nippondenso, which supplies heaters, blowers, and other parts to Honda and other Japanese automakers. Initially, Nippondenso imported these parts from their Japanese plants. But increasingly, the parts are being produced at Nippondenso's modern facility in Battle Creek, Michigan. These automakers and their suppliers help to reduce the trade deficit by producing locally the products we once imported. And they are a boon to the communities where they locate by providing employment opportunities for local workers. Foreign-made products are also helping to keep our inflation low by flooding the market with high-quality, low-cost products made right here at home.

Japanese electronics companies are moving their operations to the United States to take advantage of our relatively low labor costs and our growing markets. Sony, for example, has a large and successful assembly operation in San Diego. Sanyo and Fujitsu are producing electronics and appliances in the United States as well. In other industries, Mitsui produces more than $5 billion in plastics and animal feed additives in the United States, and Nippon Kokan is producing steel in a joint venture with National Steel Corporation. As of the end of 1985, the latest year for which complete data are available, the Japanese ministry of finance reported that Japanese investors owned at least 50 percent of 405 separate U.S. manufacturing facilities. These 405 facilities had 583 separate plants either in operation or under construction. And roughly two-thirds of the Japanese investments have been "greenfield" operations, i.e., have involved building entire new facilities with new equipment, which creates new jobs in construction and transport as well as in capital goods and manufacturing industries.

Although the Japanese presence in U.S. manufacturing is the most visible, Japan is only our third largest foreign investor and accounts for only 11 percent of all foreign direct investment in the United States. Both the British and the Dutch invest more in the United States than Japan, as chart 6.2 shows. This should not be too surprising to students of history, since the British and the Dutch financed America's first industrial revolution in the

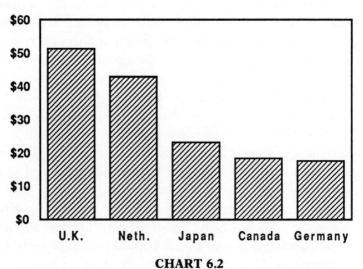

CHART 6.2
Foreign Direct Investment in the U.S. (in billions)

1800s. Their largest investments, like those of the Japanese, are concentrated in manufacturing, followed by trade and petroleum.

Recently, the flood of foreign investment coming into the United States has aroused a great amount of fear and concern that foreign investors will eventually own the whole country. Americans should remember, however, that many of the products that we now think of as household names, which are produced and consumed in America, are actually owned by foreign firms. Lipton tea is sold by a Dutch company, as are Shell gasoline and all Unilever's consumer products. Likewise, 20 Mule Team Borax is British, and Clorox bleach is German. So long as foreign firms behave as responsible corporate citizens, obey our laws, and pay their taxes, they contribute positively to our economy, offering more products to the consumer and more jobs for the worker. And as for the risk of being taken over by foreign investors, just take a look at the numbers. Based on Federal Reserve figures, we had more than $35 trillion of assets at the end of 1987 and a net worth of nearly $15 trillion. Furthermore, our $15 trillion net worth is currently growing at about $1 trillion each year, which makes the $150 to $200 billion record levels of foreign investment we have received in recent years look less menacing by comparison.

Heartland Revival

In 1982, unemployment in the United States exceeded 10 percent for the first time since the 1930s. In the industrial Midwest, things were much worse than that. Detroit had reported unemployment of 17.4 percent, and a great deal of unreported underemployment of workers who had been placed on short shifts or reduced wages. Peoria had 23 percent of its workers out of jobs in 1983 when Caterpillar Tractor, the town's largest employer, was forced to make massive layoffs. Cleveland reported 13 percent unemployment, and so on, all across America's Rust Bowl.

But things have changed. After six years of uninterrupted recovery, the second longest recovery in postwar history, the unemployment rate is now back near 5 percent. America now has the highest proportion of employed people to total population of any major industrial country, higher even than Japan. In the early stages of the recovery, essentially all the new jobs were produced by the service sector. But since early 1987, jobs in manufacturing are actually growing faster than service employment, as manufacturing companies have benefited from a growing economy and a cheaper dollar.

Detroit, more than any other city, is identified with the problems suffered by U.S. manufacturing in the 1980s. When the oil embargo hit in 1973, and people began demanding smaller cars, Detroit was slow to respond and lost a great deal of business to smaller imports. But Detroit is also where some of the biggest improvements in manufacturing have been made. Like other states in the Midwest, Michigan has actively courted investors from all around the world, offering inducements ranging from tax relief, funding for worker retraining, and road and rail improvements. Now Mazda has taken over an abandoned Ford engine plant where it assembles more than a quarter of a million engines annually, and Nippondenso has operations in Battle Creek and a research and development center in Detroit. Following the lead of Nippondenso, over seventy foreign auto-related parts and service companies have moved into the Detroit area. Civic restructuring—providing industry with the transportation, trained workers, and low tax rates they need to prosper—is just as important as corporate restructuring in promoting economic expansion and job creation.

Nearby Battle Creek suffered badly from the hard times in the auto industry and from the closing of a number of manufacturing operations in related industries.

Eaton Corporation, Clark Equipment, and Rockwell International all closed plants in Battle Creek in the early 1980s. But the town fathers created Battle Creek Unlimited, a nonprofit organization charged with promoting and managing a nearby industrial park named Fort Custer. They built roads, installed utilities and water lines, and built a cargo center with offices and warehouses. Most important, they received federal approval as a foreign trade zone, meaning there were to be no import duties on goods brought into the zone that were going to be further processed and resold abroad. They made industrial revenue bond financing, tax relief, and economic development funds available to firms moving to the facility. By 1985, thirty-eight companies had already located in the area, including four from Japan and five from Germany. Employment is growing and the downtown is being refurbished after years of decay. Civic restructuring is working in Battle Creek.

Peoria has also succeeded in coming back to life after a devastating depression that pushed the local unemployment rate to 20 percent. After receiving federal designation as a free trade zone, they were chosen as the location of Diamond Star Motors, a joint venture between Chrysler and Mitsubishi, as well as by a U.S.-Korean joint venture called Amkor Corporation, which manufactures oil filters. Meanwhile, business conditions improved for Caterpillar, thanks to the lower dollar and a rebound in farm prices. Together, foreign and domestic firms have reduced Peoria's unemployment rate to less than 8 percent, with further improvements to come.

American industry is now back on its feet. After a decade dominated by cost cutting and restructuring, American industry is now ready to build for the future again. Those who were hurt the worst, the heavy metal companies of the Midwest, are coming back the strongest. Steel, chemicals, and paper lead the pack of rapidly improving American industries. This process of rebuilding

American industry has been accelerated and aided by the inflow of foreign businesses and capital equipment, which have made our workers more productive, our costs lower, and made our products competitive again. Productivity growth in American manufacturing is higher than in any decade since the war, and has exceeded even the Japanese for the past two years. Unemployment has fallen from more than 10 percent of the work force in 1982 to just over 5 percent in 1989. But American firms will face their biggest challenge in the decade ahead. It's easy to be tough when your back is against the wall and you are fighting for survival. But will American managers have the discipline and courage to keep doing the things that made their companies healthy again, once they fall into good times? As Donald Keogh, president of Coca-Cola, told a *Business Week* reporter, "The time to be toughest is when things are going the best."

7

How to Keep T. Boone Pickens Out of Your Company

I F YOU ARE THE CHIEF EXECUTIVE OFFICER of a public company, enthroned in your regal office, complete with conference room and wet bar, there are two things that you absolutely don't want to hear your secretary say when she buzzes you on the intercom. The first is that there is a camera crew from "Sixty Minutes" in the reception area. The second is that T. Boone Pickens is holding on line one. Both calls are good for an instant case of executive heartburn, but if you absolutely had to choose between the two you would go with "Sixty Minutes." That's because if Pickens is holding on line one, you *know* why he is calling. He is calling to tell you that you have a large chunk of your company's capital tied up in low-return assets, that he has already bought a big slug of your stock, and that he wants to drop by for lunch to talk about what *we* need to do to get *our* company back in shape. That's one lunch you would like to avoid.

This chapter is for managers who absolutely, positively don't ever want to receive that phone call. There are only two ways to avoid it. The first is to have an unlisted company phone number. We do not recommend this approach, however, because it is very bad for marketing. The second is to run your company so that your shareholders get full value for their money. To do that you must keep their capital invested only in high-return businesses. That way, if Pickens were to ever present a reorganization plan to your shareholders—a plan that would reorganize you out of a fat job—they would laugh in his face. But that wouldn't happen either. Knowing that your company was in good shape, Pickens wouldn't waste his time dialing the phone.

Take care of your shareholders. It's the only way to guarantee your company's long-term independence and survival. Ultimately, whether your company is raidable or not is up to you. It is your shareholders who provide the capital you need to run the business. Your future franchise as a business, and your continued tenure as the manager of that business, depend on their continued support. And you don't win shareholder support with tricks, mirrors, or public relations campaigns. You win it with performance, by delivering superior returns on your owners' invested capital. Their support is not expressed with applause; it is expressed with money and measured in your company's stock price. Satisfying your owners, whether you run a big company or a small one, is the name of the game.

If you manage your business in a way that provides shareholders with a return on capital higher than they can earn in any other activity, you will have a lifetime franchise to manage the business. Your shareholders won't be able to afford to let you go, and your stock will be so expensive that no outside group will find it worthwhile to take you over. Nobody wants to buy a fixer upper that's already fixed—it's too expensive. And no corporate raider will pay the price it takes to buy control of a company that is already being managed for maximum performance. According to this simple philosophy, the best form of golden parachute that you can have is to manage your business so that you will never need one. Of course, managing a company for peak performance isn't easy, and it isn't all glamorous. It's a war fought every day in the trenches. And it takes a special kind of commitment from a manager who wants to win.

Blue Flame Management

Mitch Hart, our longtime friend and business adviser, is the former president of Electronic Data Systems (EDS), the computer services company founded by H. Ross Perot. We once asked Mitch whether he thought that the chief executive of a certain large bank, who was a joint acquaintance of ours, was doing a particularly good job running his company. With his Texas twang, Mitch immediately shot back, "The last time I looked he didn't have a blue flame coming out of the seat of his pants, if that answers your question."

During the 1970s, the blue flames went out all over America. Managers gave in to the temptation to structure their businesses to make easy money from inflation bets and tax shelters, as we described in chapter 2, and neglected the fundamental blocking and tackling skills they needed to keep their operating companies competitive. Tough, honest management and attention to the daily grind of product quality, customer service, cost control, and worker training, where the trench wars are fought and won running a real business, gave way to deal making as the way to make easy money. Company after company reported record profits by writing up the values of the real estate and commodity holdings on their books to reflect higher prices, while their basic businesses withered away. Blue flames were out; Learjets were in.

The good news is that blue flames are coming back in style again. The chokingly high real interest rates that hovered over our capital-short economy like a dark cloud in the 1980s have raised the ante for corporate managers, and produced a shareholder revolt in the stock market. When investors can get a 10 to 15 percent return on their money simply by clipping the interest coupons on government bonds, without having to worry about default risk, why should they be willing to risk losing their life savings financing the operations of airlines, insurance underwriters, computer companies, and other risky businesses by buying their shares in the stock market? Investors demand to do better than that, by at least enough to compensate them for the higher risks they face. Because of this higher ante, shareholders have been demanding better performance from corporate managers, and have been holding their managers' feet to the fire for higher returns. And managers, hearing the jungle drums beating in the night, have responded with a clear blue flame.

Capital is not cheap in the best of circumstances. In a capital shortage, like the one we are now experiencing in the United States, capital is extremely expensive. Having squandered immense amounts of capital building unproductive inflation hedges and tax shelters in the 1970s, we simply cannot afford to waste the precious capital resources that we still have. That means there is a premium on managers who know how to use this precious resource carefully, like Tabasco sauce in a pot of good chili. In this tough environment, complacent managers, or those whose capital management skills are not up to the higher standards demanded by today's stock market, don't survive long. In our judgment, nine out of ten takeovers are the result of somebody—usually somebody at the very top of an organization—forgetting what he's there for. A manager either forgets that he is working for the shareholders— i.e., that they are the ones who actually *own* the company—or he forgets that his concern should be profitability, not size or influence among other CEOs. In today's hardball stock market, either form of amnesia can be terminal for the forgetful manager.

One of the most popular theories circulating among the business schools during the 1970s was the concept that shareholder ownership and control had become outdated and no longer applied to the large, complex, modern corporation. Instead, they claimed, a corporation actually has many *stakeholders*, including the shareholders, the workers, the customers, civic and charitable groups, and even various government entities, none of whom deserve special treatment over the others. It is the job of the manager, they claimed, to balance the conflicting interests of all the different stakeholders of the business somehow, like a judge in a courtroom, rather than single out any particular one for special treatment.

Since the judge sits on a level higher than anyone else in the courtroom and has final say in deciding who gets what out of the company coffers, this idea became very popular in the boardrooms across the country. It made the professional manager, not the shareholder, the central figure in deciding which of his many constituencies should be next at the trough, and turned him into a commercial version of the politician. Best of all, it seemed to let the manager off the hook on his most difficult assignment— producing consistently higher returns for his shareholders than they can earn on competing uses of their capital. Echoing these words of pseudo-wisdom, one prominent CEO, while engaged in a battle to fend off an uninvited takeover offer, explained in legislative hearings that it wouldn't be right to let the lives and fortunes of the company's loyal managers, workers, suppliers, and customers be affected by the fickle whims of shareholders who might have only owned his stock for fifteen minutes.

What he forgot to mention is that the shareholder, even if he only bought the stock fifteen minutes ago, paid good money for it that the CEO is now using to run the business. Moreover, the new shareholder took the place of a previous shareholder, who owned the stock before, and so on, all the way back to the day the company was founded. Someone has to own the company's stock at all times. Without those shareholders, the manager would have no business at all. And if shareholders were to lose their traditional role as the providers of discipline to their managers, rewarding managers when they do a good job and replacing them when they don't, who would take their place? Further, as Peter Drucker has forcefully written for the past half century, companies that are unable to produce consistent profits for their shareholders over the long term don't do a very good job for their other stakeholders either. Workers, managers, customers, and suppliers all do better when a company is profitable and growing than when it is stagnant and dying. Fortunately, the shareholder revolt of the 1980s has driven the idea of nonaccountability back into the ivory tower where it will do a lot less damage to our businesses.

Did you ever wonder why you don't hear much about hostile takeovers of private companies? It's not because private companies are inherently unraidable. It doesn't take much imagination to figure out what would happen if a new management team convinced Aunt Agnes, the controlling shareholder of Acme Nuts and Bolts, that they could triple the company's long-term profits, and her dividend checks, by making a few management changes. The company's current management, even if it were headed by her favorite nephew, Harold, would be out on the street with a résumé in a New York minute. Blood may be thicker than water, but more often than not money is even thicker than blood. In principle, private companies are easier to raid than public companies, not harder, because there are usually so few owners in a private company that you can call them all up and sit down with them over a beer to talk over your ideas for improving their business. The expensive proxy battles that must be waged to wrest control of a publicly owned company with thousands of absentee shareholders from an entrenched management are much harder to pull off.

The reason you don't hear of many takeovers of privately owned companies is simply that the opportunity doesn't arise very often, because private companies are run better than public companies. Not always, but usually. Since the entire rationale for taking over a company is to make substantial improvements in the company's return on capital, a company that is already squeezing every last drop of profits out of shareholder capital simply doesn't make a very interesting takeover target.

The distinction between public and private companies is one of involvement vs. commitment. To illustrate the difference, the chicken's relationship with the egg is one of involvement, but the pig is irreversibly committed to the bacon. In a private company, the manager is committed just like the pig and the bacon. He knows that his own capital is at risk every day. He is intensely interested in the company's success, and cannot even consider the possibility of failure. For owners of private companies, changing jobs is not an option when the business goes into a tailspin. If the company fails, he goes down the smokestack with it.

For the past several years we have written a monthly column on the subject of business and investments. Looking back over the columns dealing with successful businesses, we find a story about Stone Manufacturing, a family-owned garment company in Greenville, South Carolina, another about the Roulston Company, a class-act brokerage firm in Cleveland, and another about Exchange Bank, a small, privately owned bank in northern California. In fact, the only repeat characteristic of all the companies we had singled out to write about as star performers was that they were either privately owned or companies where the managers owned a substantial stake in the future of the business.

Private companies tend to be managed better than public companies because in a private company the owner and the manager are usually the same person. That leaves very little room for owner-manager conflict of interest, and even less room for managerial politics. And it gives private company managers a whole different perspective on cost controls. When the owner-manager of a private business pays too much for an airline ticket, the money comes out of his own pocket. We know, we own a company ourselves. That's why you can usually find these authors sitting with the other private company owners in the coach section of the airplane. If you're looking for the public company executives, you'll have to walk up front to the first-class compartment. Not coincidentally, most of the managers that we know who regularly walk around with blue flames coming out of the seat of their pants work for private companies or own substantial interests in their companies. That may be why more than 80 percent of the new jobs created in America in the past decade have been in small, private companies.

There are some terrific public companies, too. These tend to be the ones where the managers run the companies as if they were the owners. But this is a real accomplishment when it happens, because it's a lot easier for the owner of a private company to get fired up to make profits—he's too scared even to think of failing. So it is impressive when you see public companies that are being managed in the same tough way that many private companies are run. From our observations over the past ten years, General Electric, as we have already cited, may be the best-managed large company in America today. They know what they are there for, delivering steady and growing profits to their shareholders, and they are not afraid to do what's needed to make it happen. Yet GE has been a public company since the days of Edison. And, through force of example, hard work, and personal commitment, Robert Crandall has been able to create the same atmosphere among the managers of American Airlines, even during the chaotic deregulation period of the 1980s that tore many of American's competitors apart. We are great admirers of these companies. Unfortunately, companies like GE and American are the exception not the rule among large publicly owned companies.

Based on our travels among the boardrooms of hundreds of companies, we are happy to report that the most dramatic improvements in management are taking place where they are needed most, among public companies in our industrial sector. That's important news for our economy because so much of our capital is invested in and controlled by large companies. There is an invisible force at work that is putting pressure on the managers of public companies to behave more like privately owned operations. Whether you call it a shareholder revolt, corporate raiders, leveraged buyouts, or simply a more competitive capital market, something has created a shotgun marriage atmosphere that has captured the hearts and minds of corporate America.

One CEO we know expressed it this way: "The breakup value of your company is like a cloud that you can always see over your shoulder—it's always there and no matter what you do, you can never get away from it. You know that if you allow your stock price to dip too far below that number, you're dead in the water. I'm not going to let that happen to me."

Corporate raiders, arbitrageurs, and active shareholders are not inherently good or bad, they are simply a part of the landscape in an economy that is scratching for every dollar of capital it needs to grow. But they are forcing important changes in the way our businesses are being managed, forcing every manager to decide whether he wants to learn to play hardball or get out of business. Remember, the CEO we described above may be your biggest competitor.

PRINCIPLE ONE   Blue flame management is no longer an elective. It is a required course. Today you need to be a blue flame manager just to keep your head above water.

Capital is scarce and very expensive. There is intense competition among management teams for the right to manage a business. As a manager, you must prove every day that you deserve the job of calling the shots on allocating a portion of our economy's scarce financial resources. To maintain your role as steward of your shareholders' dollars, you must *commit* your management team's efforts to producing consistently superior returns for your owners, and to fighting the daily trench war to build and run a successful company.

But blue flame management means more than working hard; it means working smart. Showing up at the office earlier, staying later, and walking around the office with a blue flame all day will set a good example for your troops, but it won't necessarily make your business run better. You have to know how to direct your work toward improving your shareholders' returns on capital, and that means managing your company's assets just as intensively as you manage your revenues and your costs. The next section tells you how to use the perspective of an outsider to help manage the assets of your business.

Be Your Own Raider

Running a business has always been a full-time job. In today's demanding business climate there are so many conflicting pressures on the chief executive that the job is all but impossible. Most managers spend all their time up to their you-know-whats in alligators, just handling their day-to-day problems, and never get a chance to step back and look at their businesses objectively, as an outsider would. They do things this year because they did them last year, without asking whether they should be doing them at all. This *managerial momentum* can be very expensive, because an outsider is often able to look at a company with the cold eye of a surgeon, deciding which assets are worth keeping and which assets are dead weight and a net drag on the company's profits. And the more dead weight the company carries, the cheaper its stock will be, and the easier it will be for another management team to take over the company.

Fortunately, this is an easy problem to cure. All you have to do is climb out of the pit of daily operations at regular intervals, mentally step outside of your own company, and be your own raider. Place yourself in the role of an outside buyer taking a look at your company as a possible acquisition. After you have looked the place over, kick the tires and appraise the operations. You will get a good idea whether your company is raidable, i.e., if there is a way to reorganize the business to make it worth more than it will cost you to buy it. If so, put on your ten-gallon Boone Pickens hat, call a meeting of your senior managers, and say, "Boys, I've decided this company is raidable, and I'm the raider. Now tell me what *we* are going to do to get *our* business back in shape." If you're tough enough, and make them sit through the squirming stage until the profitable, but unpleasant, ideas show up on the table, you'll uncover all sorts of ways to improve the value of your company. And you'll find that it is much more pleasant being on the ten-gallon-hat side of the table than wringing your hands in the executive washroom, waiting for the phone to ring.

The key to thinking like a raider is to recognize that you are running two different businesses. You have an *operating company*, where you hire workers, make products, and record monthly profits and losses. It is the one measured by your monthly profit-and-loss statements. And you run a *portfolio company*, which holds a portfolio of inventories, working capital, and fixed assets, such as machines and office buildings, and where you record your obligations to the bank, to your bondholders, and to your stockholders. It is the one measured by your balance sheet.

The key to profitability is maintaining the appropriate balance between your operating company and your balance sheet, holding just enough assets on your books to meet the needs of your operating company, but not so many as to drown your company in obligations to your bondholders and stockholders. In the 1970s it became fashionable for companies to fatten up their balance sheets and increase the size of their asset base relative to their operating company by borrowing money or issuing new shares. They would then use the new funds to acquire stockpiles of commodities, real estate, or other fixed assets in the name of hedging the company against inflation. But often, by the time management had finished "hedging" their business against inflation, there was little left of the original business to recognize. This amounted to little more than a straight gamble of shareholder money on the prices of the assets they were buying, since there was no way the operating company could generate sufficient profits to adequately service the company's creditors, its bondholders, and still pay its shareholders an adequate return on their investment. They were watering the stock to play the ponies.

It is inappropriate for business managers to gamble their shareholders' capital on expected changes in fixed-asset prices. Borrowing money to buy things in the hopes their prices will go up should be left to the professional portfolio managers; it has nothing to do with running a business. Instead, the business manager's job is to refine the performance of the operating company so as to produce a steady stream of long-term profits, and to do it with as little capital as possible. The balance sheet should be managed to support the activities of the operating company, not as a business of its own, and it should be as small as reasonably possible in order to raise returns and to free up capital for other profitable pursuits.

Most companies own more assets than they need to run their businesses. That's understandable, because a business accumulates a certain amount of "stuff" from year to year in the normal course of business. First you needed a typewriter. Then IBM came out with a model with a memory and a self-correcting ribbon. Then you bought the word processor to increase clerical productivity. Now you are thinking of replacing it with a faster model. Each move made sense when you made it because it allowed your people to do a lot more work than they could do with the previous technology. But we'll bet there is a closet or a storeroom in your company—a managerial version of the elephants' burial ground—where you will still find all the old machines gathering dust. That's understandable, too; it's a lot easier to buy things than sell them when they are used. But it also drags down your returns. The unused assets that are lying around your storeroom are still on your company's books, fattening up your asset base and watering down your return on capital.

The smart thing to do is to have a garage sale, get rid of all the stuff that is lying around, and give the money back to your shareholders. This will reduce the capital your shareholders have invested in the business and raise their future return on equity (ROE), even if your future profits don't rise by one cent. (ROE is calculated by dividing profits by the value of shareholders' equity—if you can find a way to shrink shareholders' equity without reducing profits, ROE will rise.) Give it a try. We think you'll agree that it's a lot less work to have a garage sale than to find a way to increase your profits every year for the rest of your life. That's what we mean by working smart.

This advice is just as useful for small businesses as for big ones. In the past year we have helped one very big business find ways to unload nearly a billion dollars of low-return assets, which amounted to about a quarter of their total book value, and then give the money back to its shareholders through a massive share repurchase program. And they were able to do it without meaningfully reducing their profits. This increased their return on equity by more than 20 percent. We saw a tiny family-owned business avoid insolvency by selling a used car and several pieces of discarded equipment that were filling up a corner of their storeroom, using the proceeds to pay their most pressing debts. Most businesses manage their assets so poorly that they pay 10 to 15 percent interest to the bank each month on the loans they use to finance their inventories and receivables, while earning no interest at all on the underused assets sitting around collecting dust in the closet. Trying to run a profitable business while holding a bloated balance sheet is like trying to win a race while pulling a sled. For many businesses, the cheapest source of new capital may be their own closet.

Many managers spend all their energy trying to wring the last drop of costs out of an already lean operation while the answer to their problem lies right in front of them. At least half the battle in building a profitable business has nothing to do with the price of the product or the operating costs of the business. It is determined by a business's *capital turnover,* or how many dollars of sales it manages to generate per dollar of capital tied up in the business—essentially a measure of how hard the assets of the company are working to earn their keep.

The right way to measure the success of a business enterprise, as we discussed above, is its profitability—i.e., profits per dollar of capital. The most useful way to measure this is to divide the profits of the business by the amount of equity tied up in the business. This is, as we discussed above, the return on equity, or ROE.

$$ROE = profits/equity$$

As the following formula shows, however, the ROE is jointly determined by both the profit margin and by the rate at which the company turns over its equity capital.

$$ROE = profits/sales \times sales/equity$$

Profits per dollar of sales is simply the business's profit margin, and sales per dollar of equity is capital turnover, so:

$$\text{ROE} = \text{profit margin} \times \text{capital turnover}$$

So increasing the turnover of a company's capital is just as powerful as raising the profit margin as a way to improve shareholder returns. And sometimes it is a darn sight easier to accomplish, since it can be done inside the business, it does not force you to fire anyone, and it does not require renegotiating prices with your customers or your suppliers.

Some companies are using what is called the *sale-leaseback* as a way to speed up the turnover of their asset base. They have figured out that they don't really need to own their office building to run their business. So they are making arrangements to sell the building to an investor and lease it back for their own use. This technique is partly an accounting gimmick—by selling the asset today for an amount greater than its value on the company's books, the company gets a shot in the arm to the current year's earnings, at the cost of reducing future earnings by the amount of the lease payments. And it is partially a tax gimmick, since it allows a company to change the profile of its earnings over time to make the most out of different tax rates on capital gains and ordinary income, or different tax rates from one tax year to the next. But it also reduces the company's assets, and therefore *increases* capital turnover. Finally, the ongoing lease payments help to force a company's management to face the music that the use of an office building involves an ongoing cost to the business, whether or not it is owned by the company. Our favorite strategy of all is the *sale-no-leaseback*, where you sell the building, give the money back to shareholders or use it to reduce your debts, and move into smaller, cheaper quarters.

Remember, as we will see below, your objective as a manager is not just to produce high profits, it is to produce consistently high profits per dollar of invested capital used to support the business. The return on capital can be improved both by raising profits and by finding ways to run the business with less capital. Every dollar of fat carried around on your company's balance sheet makes it that much more difficult to achieve your objectives.

PRINCIPLE TWO   Learn to be your own raider. Managerial momentum is your worst enemy. You must stand outside your business and evaluate it as a potential buyer, looking for opportunities to raise capital turnover, identifying which assets you really need to run your business, selling the rest, and reducing your capital base to the solid, and unraidable, core.

Profitability, Not Profits

Many managers believe their job is to make as much profit as possible for their shareholders, and that all strategies that increase total profits will be good for the company. Based on this criterion, General Motors looks like a screaming success. In 1987, GM racked up nearly $3.2 billion in profits on total sales of almost $102 billion, an increase of 22 percent from the profits they earned in 1986. Yet their 1987 price-to-book-value multiple—a good measure of shareholder confidence in management's ability to deliver profits in the future—was only 0.85, compared with an average of 2.22 for the more than 900 companies summarized in the Value Line Industrial Composite (VLIC). And GM's price-earnings ratio, another measure of shareholder satisfaction with the way the business is being run, was only 7, about half that of the average company in the market. Part of GM's problem was that its return on equity, at 11.5 percent, was less than the 12.5 percent market average for 1987. But more important was the fact that GM's U.S. market share had dropped by 20 percent since the beginning of the 1980s, and the growing sentiment that GM was not up to competing with the new Japanese transplants—new factories to produce Hondas, Toyotas, and other foreign-nameplate cars on American soil—that were popping up like mushrooms all over the country. Clearly, GM shareholders were unimpressed with GM's $3.2 billion in profits; they were interested in GM's returns per dollar of capital over the long haul. And they didn't like what they saw.

You don't have to be big or make billions of dollars in profits to get top marks from your shareholders. Wal-Mart Stores, whose 1987 book value—their net plant, equipment, and other assets valued at historical cost—of $2.3 billion was less than GM's profits for the same year, earned $628 million in profits for a return on equity of 28 percent. And Wal-Mart's sales, profits, and book value have all grown more than 35 percent per year for the past ten years! Shareholders, including insiders who own more than 40 percent of the stock, are so pleased with management's performance that at the end of 1987 the stock had a market value of nearly eight times its book value, making the company's stock worth $17.8 billion.

Sears, Roebuck, despite its massive $13.6 billion in book value, made only $1.6 billion in profits in 1987, for an ROE of 12.1 percent. Its ten-year profit and book-value growth rates were only 6 percent. Sears' mediocre performance, high costs—Sears' overhead costs per dollar of sales run about twice as high as those of Wal-Mart—and declining market share have not won the admiration of their shareholders. In 1987, Sears, Roebuck stock sold for only 1.19 times their book value. So giant Sears' stock was worth only $16 billion in the stock market, 9 percent less than the much smaller but more profitable Wal-Mart. If I were managing Sears, and I wanted to keep my job until retirement, I would start cutting overhead and reducing the company's assets in a hurry.

WD-40, the company that makes the well-known lubricant and rust remover, has been phenomenally profitable for many years. With only $32.8 million in book value in 1987, WD-40 earned $11 million in profits, for a phenomenal 33.6 percent return on shareholders' equity. The company's dependable ROE numbers—30 percent is a bad year at WD-40—and its 22 percent annual book-value growth rate for the past ten years have also earned the company a stock price of eight times book value, and have made the tiny $32.8 million in shareholder equity worth a quarter of a billion dollars in the stock market! This means that if General Motors were to approach the WD-40 shareholders with an offer to buy the company by exchanging shares at book value, WD-40 shareholders would lose 90 percent of their money if they accepted the deal. Needless to say, the managers of WD-40 aren't losing sleep worrying about corporate raiders and hostile takeovers.

PRINCIPLE THREE   When evaluating business plans, it is profitability—the return on each dollar of capital—not profits that counts in producing shareholder value. The rate of return per dollar of invested capital depends on both the performance of your business and the amount of capital you use to run it. That means you should operate your business with as little capital as possible, not as much as possible. And it means that you should think twice before you accept additional capital from investors. Unless you are able to invest the additional capital in projects that will have returns at least as high as those in your core business, more capital will simply dilute shareholder returns, weaken your business, and make your company more vulnerable to outside attack.

Peeling the Artichoke

Most businesses are like an artichoke. At the heart of the business there is usually a terrific product or business line that has historically been very profitable. But it is usually surrounded by so many layers of junk that you're not sure if it is worth the effort. The job of the manager is to keep relentlessly pulling off the outer leaves of the artichoke until he has exposed the valuable heart of the business. The heart of the business is what your shareholders will pay you to manage.

One company we know was having a difficult time making enough profits to satisfy their shareholders. Their return on equity averaged less than 8 percent, compared with more than 12 percent for the average company in the stock market. Not too surprisingly, their stock price suffered, selling well below the value of their assets. Since this company was a financial services firm whose assets were largely held as government bonds—which could be sold at full value at a minute's notice—this made them a sitting duck for the first takeover artist to stroll down the block.

They had done all the obvious things to improve their profits, their CEO told us, including cutting their overhead to the bone. And they were charging the highest prices for their products they thought they could get away with. But still they weren't very profitable. What could they do?

The solution to the problem was simple. What they thought of as one business with low returns was actually a ragbag of different businesses and product lines that had been pasted together over the years, all with different operating characteristics and different rates of return. Looking at their various operations separately, we were surprised to learn that about a third of the company's profits came from the company's core business—the one with which they had made their name over the years. This business enjoyed a virtual monopoly in a particular niche, with an ROE of more than 60 percent. It doesn't take much to figure out that if the core of the company is earning a 60 percent return, and the company as a whole, *including* the core business, is earning an 8 percent return, something is not pulling its weight. The answer to their problem was simple: Start pulling off the artichoke's leaves and throw away the tough, low-return, outer businesses until they got to the sweet center.

PRINCIPLE FOUR   The purpose of restructuring is to pull off the artichoke's leaves and eliminate less lucrative business units and product lines in search of the profitable core. Divide your company into separate business units, allocate capital to each unit and rank them by return on capital. By purging low-return activities you can substantially raise your company's returns.

Know When to Stop

It takes two people to make a great painting, the story goes, one to paint it and the other to tell him when it is done. The same goes for building, restructuring, and running a business. Restructuring a business is like getting a haircut when you know your hair is too long. The basic idea is to cut it shorter, but unless you like the Yul Brynner look the trick is knowing when to stop.

The chairman of one Fortune 500 corporation, after a meeting in which we had advised him that his company was not profitable enough to keep his stock price at an acceptable level—i.e., that his company was badly in need of a haircut—expressed his frustrations in the following words: "We have been restructuring this company every day now for five years," he said. "We have reduced our work force by more than sixteen thousand people, slashed our overhead, and sold more than $700 million in assets.

We have sold, scrapped, or closed down forty-two businesses. We have turned our core business inside out and rebuilt it from the ground up, streamlined our operations, and pruned nearly half of our distributors. There's not a single area of this company that we haven't been over. And yet all that we have managed to do so far is to go from being lousy to mediocre, moving from the bottom of our peer group to the middle, and raising our return on equity from five percent to ten percent. I know that's not good enough, but if I go back to my senior managers and ask them to cut one more time, I'm not sure they even have the energy to hear me blow the bugle."

The problem was that for the previous five years he had continually exhorted his troops to do better, but he hadn't given them a measurable target so they would know when they were done. It was like asking a group of managers to keep pushing a big rock around a field without telling them where they are going. There is no way to celebrate success unless you know when you have achieved victory.

The goal of restructuring a company should be to increase shareholder value. Everybody knows that getting rid of low-return businesses, and either returning the proceeds to shareholders or reinvesting it in high-return businesses creates shareholder value. And getting rid of high-return businesses destroys shareholder value. But how high is high, and how low is low? Where is the cutoff between good businesses and bad businesses that will help a manager know how far he has to cut? The answer is that *the manager needs to cut out all of the businesses that have returns lower than the firm's cost of capital.*

The cost of capital, the return demanded by the company's investors, serves as a draftsman's straightedge to help guide a chief executive in knowing how much of a business to cut, and how much to keep. Having a well-defined cutoff for a company's profitability makes a manager's job a lot easier. As an illustration, put yourself in the size seventeen sneakers of a basketball coach the first day of training camp, looking over the new year's group of hopeful future stars. His job will be a lot tougher if the general manager tells him to "get rid of the short guys" than if he's told to cut every player shorter than six feet. In either case, of course, he is going to need to line the players up against the wall and rank them by height in order to do his job. But in the second case he will know exactly where he has to make the cut.

It is not easy to determine the precise cost of capital for a given company. But a useful rule of thumb is to double the long-term government bond rate, which would make the cost of capital for most businesses between 15 and 20 percent. So a manager restructuring his company should cut out all businesses that do not have a reasonable prospect of achieving a 15 percent return on equity over the next several years.

PRINCIPLE FIVE   The most important part of restructuring is knowing when to stop. When you have stripped away all businesses with returns lower than your company's cost of capital (about 15 percent for many businesses), stop the music. Even a good thing can be carried too far. Cutting business activities with returns higher than your cost of capital means cutting muscle, not fat. Further cutting will reduce the value of your company.

Capital Budgeting

We have learned over the years that ideas are cheap. It is the act of following through on them that creates value. The same goes for the ideas we have discussed in this chapter. Nodding your head at all the right places is one thing, but unless you find a way to build them into the discipline of running your business, they won't help you at all.

The first step in implementing these ideas is to perform a self-audit of your company's capital. This means identifying the capital you have committed to different activities and estimating the returns that can be earned on the capital in each activity. Next, rank them by return, from highest to lowest. The top of your list will be your star performers, the unraidable core of your business. The ones on the bottom are candidates for surgery. Slice the list at the 15 percent ROE level, and put all the businesses that fall below the line on probation. Ask the managers of each business to come up with a plan to raise its returns above the line within a reasonable period, or to come up with other reasons why the business should not be sold. If the business fails to get off the probation list for three years in a row, take a close look at it. It may be a turkey that would be better off in someone else's barnyard.

In summary, the steps that should be followed to implement a capital budgeting system to improve your company's asset management and increase shareholder returns are the following:

1. Agree on a goal. Creating shareholder value, which means only undertaking investments for which the rate of return exceeds the company's cost of capital, is a good place to start.

2. Agree on a yardstick. For most businesses, return on shareholders' equity over a three-to-five-year period is a useful way to measure management performance.

3. Agree on a minimum standard of performance, based on estimates of your company's cost of capital.

4. Audit current businesses. Identify the capital you have committed to each business or product. Rank the businesses by return, from highest to lowest.

5. Establish procedures for pruning poor performers. Place businesses that fall below the line on probation, and either improve their performance or get rid of them in a reasonable period.

6. Do it again every year. Pruning and shaping a business is like weeding a garden. If you turn your back too long, the weeds will grow back and overrun your garden.

7. Create incentives for top performance. Don't forget that if your efforts are to succeed somebody is going to have to do the work. Regardless of the boardroom rhetoric, if your managers don't enthusiastically support your business plan, nothing is going to happen. Make sure that you aren't talking shareholder returns while paying your managers bonuses based on sales, asset size, or other measures of company performance that may be in conflict with profitability. Create incentives for your managers so they do well when, and only when, the shareholders do well.

PRINCIPLE SIX   Install and implement a capital budgeting system to run parallel with your annual budgeting cycle. Talking about creating a high-return business is great fun, but it won't improve your returns a dime. You have to actually do it, all day, every day, to make it work.

8

Looking Back on the 1990s

"Is there any point to which you would like to draw my attention?" asked Inspector LeStrade.

"To the curious incident of the dog in the night-time."

"The dog did nothing in the night-time."

"That was the curious incident," remarked Sherlock Holmes.

The Curious Incident of the Dog in the Nighttime

SOMETIMES WHAT PEOPLE DON'T SEE can be more revealing than what they do see, as Sherlock Holmes explained to Inspector LeStrade in "Silver Blaze." Likewise, students of economics in the twenty-first century, when looking at the history of the massive change that swept across the American economy during the 1980s and 1990s, will find curious what the experts did not see. Economists, political leaders, and the financial press have spent the whole time wringing their hands about America's intractable budget and trade deficits. They failed to see the changes that were taking place around them until it was too late to avoid the problems and exploit the opportunities presented by economic change, either for running businesses or investing money.

Those students will wonder how it could have been possible for economists to observe the total transformation of the American economy without seeing what was happening right in front of their noses—from the tax shelter and inflation hedge binge that preoccupied American investors during the 1970s, through the deflation and restructuring of our manufacturing companies in the 1980s, and into a decade of productivity growth and expansion without inflation in the 1990s (including the longest period without a recession in recorded history). For while these changes were taking place, the experts had joined voices in a chorus of impending doom, worrying about the inflation and economic collapse that were never to come.

Yogi Berra once said, "You can observe a lot just by watching." But effective watching requires both open eyes and an open mind. Unfortunately, most people are only able to see what their beliefs and assumptions *allow* them to see. This is because we use our beliefs about how the world works to help us screen out the extraneous noise—in the same way we use sunglasses to screen out glaring sunlight—so we can focus on the few facts that are really important to help make sense out of what we see taking place in the world around us. Moreover, people fear what they don't understand. Long ago, for example, the scholars were certain that the earth was flat. So when people saw a ship slowly disappear over the horizon they worried that it had fallen off the edge of the earth. We don't worry about such things today because today it is accepted wisdom that the earth is round and gravity holds us to it, so we *expect* to see objects disappear as they approach the horizon.

Thus, when the facts we observe don't fit neatly into our accepted explanations, we often try to bend them until they do or else we say, "This doesn't make sense in my logical framework, therefore it cannot last." But often the anomaly is not with the facts; it is with our interpretation of the facts, and our understanding about how the world works.

Like Chicken Little in the fairy tale, economists today

are worried that the sky is falling because the events of the 1980s don't fit neatly into any of the little boxes provided by the textbooks. This is quite understandable when viewed from the perspective of an orthodox macroeconomist who believes that all that is interesting in the economy originates as a disturbance to one of the components of spending in the national income accounts, and that the principal forces behind changes in economic growth are changes in government spending. To such an economist, the 1980s must seem like an unsolvable riddle of inconsistencies. In the textbooks, rising budget deficits are supposed to push interest rates higher, but in the 1980s, big deficits have been accompanied by *falling* interest rates. Large trade deficits are supposed to "export jobs," but during the period of swollen budget deficits the economy has created an incredible 15 million new jobs and unemployment rates have fallen to the lowest levels in fifteen years. Business-cycle watchers keep telling us we are "overdue" for a recession, but for seven years now, like ol' man river, economic growth just keeps rolling along. And in spite of all this growth, falling unemployment rates, and a declining dollar, inflation rates have remained generally low, defying the traditional logic of the Phillips Curve—the idea that there is an immutable tradeoff between the evils of inflation and unemployment.

It is not surprising, however, that what has happened in the 1980s is inconsistent with textbook macroeconomics, which focuses on spending and income flows and all but ignores the economy's capital structure. The driving forces behind economic change in the 1980s were not changes in government spending or in the public's propensity to spend. Instead, as we described in chapter 2, massive changes in the country's capital structure turned the asset markets inside out, played havoc with the net worth of individuals and companies, and brought about the repricing, restructuring, and rebuilding of literally trillions of dollars in capital assets! The textbooks didn't prepare economists of the 1980s for anything like that.

But the sky is not falling. It's just the clouds that are moving. The changes of the 1980s, even though they were difficult for many businesses and individuals, will have extremely positive effects on the economy for years to come. Disinflation, reduced tax rates, and the repeal of tax shelters, not budget and trade deficits, were the real motor forces behind economic change in the 1980s. Initially, disinflation and tax reform caused a great deal of turmoil in the economy by forcing managers and investors to face up to the damage that inflation and tax shelters had done to our capital resources during the 1970s. But in the 1980s, disinflation and tax reform forced investors to write off hundreds of billions of dollars of inflated real estate, oil, farmland, and other tangible assets, and we were con- fronted with the fact that our factories and machines were too old and inefficient to allow us to compete with man- ufacturers in other countries. Happily, most American managers faced these problems head-on by restructuring their companies to reduce costs and raise productivity, by building more capital goods at home, and by importing capital from abroad. And this has laid the foundation for a decade of solid growth and low inflation in the 1990s.

Common sense tells us there are only two questions worth asking when trying to forecast a country's future living standards. Do the people want to work? Do they have the tools they need to make their work productive? If people have the incentive to work and the proper tools to work with, they will find a way to get the job done. Unfortunately, we started the 1980s with poor marks in both areas. High tax rates in the 1970s worked like novocaine to deaden people's work incentives. A destruc- tive tax code had undermined the link between effort and reward, and had channeled a great amount of people's time and energy away from efforts to create wealth and toward efforts to avoid paying taxes. Moreover, inflation and tax shelters had diverted our savings dollars into the construction of new hotels, office buildings, and shopping centers instead of new factories and new tools for our industrial workers.

Dangers Still Ahead

Of course, low inflation and tax reform have not solved our economic problems for all time. We are still vulnerable to wars, crop failures, oil supply interruptions, and overzealous Federal Reserve chairmen. But to borrow Mark Twain's words, the greatest dangers that still lie before us come from that "grand old asylum for the inept," the U.S. Congress, and the possibility that it might raise taxes. It is no secret that most members of Congress are drooling over the prospect of collecting more tax revenues. That way they could avoid the need to cut their favorite spending programs. The second danger is another outbreak of congressional trade bashing—protectionism is very popular with the voters back home. But higher taxes and protectionism would undermine the foundations of prosperity that we paid so dearly to put in place. Higher tax rates would undermine work and savings incentives by decreasing the amount that a worker actually got to bring home to his family out of each dollar earned. And, in the same way a rainstorm raises the value of umbrellas, higher tax rates would increase the value of tax shelters again. This would reawaken the destructive tax shelter industry and redirect our scarce stream of savings dollars away from factories and machines and into building the "wrong stuff," just as we did in the 1970s. But higher tax rates, as Yogi Berra said, would be like "déjà vu all over again."

Likewise, protectionism would also be very destructive for the American economy. As we showed in chapter 5, the trade deficit has not been made up of Hondas, BMWs, and Sonys, as most people believe. On the contrary, it is mostly capital equipment and industrial supplies—the same stuff that built the new Honda plant in Marysville, Ohio, and the same stuff that is raising the productivity and lowering the costs of manufacturing companies all across America. Without new tools, American industry will not be able to compete for a share of expanding markets overseas, let alone win back customers here at home. And foreign capital is helping American consumers, too, by increasing our capacity to produce goods at a reasonable price. Protectionism would only force American consumers to pay higher prices for lower living standards.

The Stock Market: 5,000 in 2000

If we can count on our Congress and President Bush to hold the line on both taxes and free trade, one of the things we can expect is continued improvement in the stock market. It may seem courageous to predict that the Dow Jones Industrial Average, which was below 800 in mid-1982 and has been bouncing around the 2,000 mark for the past year, will climb all the way to 5,000 by the turn of the century, only eleven years away. Especially for those who witnessed the spectacular stock market crash on October 19, 1987, when the Dow Jones Industrial Average dropped more than 500 points in a single day. The fact is, however, a Dow Jones Industrial Average of 5,000 by the turn of the century would represent little more than cruise control, merely a continuation of long-term stock market historical trends. For example, stock prices rose so much in the first nine months of 1987 that an investor who purchased a broadly diversified portfolio of stocks on January 1, 1987, and held them for a full year, including the period of the October crash, would have registered a positive 5 percent return when he sold them a year later!

According to legend, when a reporter once asked J. P. Morgan what the stock market would do in the following year, he replied, "It will fluctuate." Indeed, since Morgan's time the market has "fluctuated" through a depression and many recessions as well as quite a few boom years. But in general, it has fluctuated up. In fact, over the long haul, the up years far outweigh the down years, and long-term investors are well rewarded for their patience. As the following table shows, small company stocks have paid investors an incredible 18.2 percent average annual return for the past sixty years—their pay for enduring the roller-coaster ride of small company earnings. But the return on the overall stock market, which includes the large, stable blue chip companies such as IBM and General Electric, hasn't been bad either— even after inflation, which averaged only 3.1 percent over this sixty-year period, the *real* return for the stock market has been about 9 percent per year, including both dividends and appreciation, compared with the 0.4 percent real return on Treasury bills. For an investor who had diligently reinvested his dividends over the full sixty-year period, that's enough to have doubled the real value of an average investor's portfolio every eight years since 1926.

But 5,000 in 2000? The following simple analysis shows it's not only possible, but quite likely. Since the 12.1 percent annual total return on stocks includes dividend income, which averaged about 4 percent per year, we can see that stock prices have increased at about 8 percent per year, on average, for the past six decades. Because of the miracle of compound interest, a number growing at 8 percent per year will double in just nine years. That means if the stock market just duplicates its average historical performance and grows by 8 percent per year for the rest of the century, the Dow Jones Industrial Average would double in value, from about 2,200 at the beginning of 1989 to 4,400 nine years later, at the beginning of 1998. And the

Dow would stand at 5,132 two years later, on New Year's Day in the year 2000!

Of course, these are averages, and everybody knows you can't walk across a river just because it is only 3 feet deep on average. That's why the stock market is not a good place to invest your rent money. It only makes sense for long-term investors who can take their lumps, or for short-term gamblers who like the excitement. As the risk measure—which measures how much higher or lower than the average return an investor is likely to experience in a given year—in the right-hand column of table 4 shows, the returns on stocks are substantially riskier than on most other types of financial investments, two and a half times more risky than corporate or government bonds, and six times more risky than the returns on Treasury bills. The stock market is no place for widows and orphans who need steady, dependable income. It is for investors who have the luxury of taking the long view.

Still, 5,000 in 2000 is not a scary bet at all. In fact, we believe stocks will do a lot better than that. The economic forces that have led to the reindustrialization of America have forced dramatic changes in the way American industrial managers are running their companies, changes that are showing up as improvements in the productivity,

TABLE 4 Returns on Alternative Investments: 1926–1986

Investment	Total Return (Percent)	Real Return (Percent)	Risk (Percent)
Small stocks	18.2	15.1	36.0
Stocks	12.1	9.0	21.2
Corporate bonds	5.3	2.2	8.5
Government bonds	4.7	1.6	8.6
Treasury bills	3.5	0.4	3.4
Inflation	3.1	0	4.9

Source: Ibbotson Associates

profits, and cash flows of our companies. Those fundamental improvements in business performance will be reflected in higher stock prices just as they have been all through history. But the forces pushing stock prices higher in the 1990s will be much different from those that produced the bull market of the 1980s. Understanding those differences is crucial for picking which stocks to own in the years ahead.

The Free Lunch Is Over

In the 1980s, if you were warm and had the energy to pick up the telephone to call your broker, you made money in the stock market. In a market that began at 780 in 1982 and rose more or less steadily to 2,000, it would have taken a serious effort to select a portfolio that lost money if held over the whole period. The secret to smart investing in the 1980s was not deciding which stock to buy, it was deciding to be in the market at all. Those who were in the market all through the decade of the 1980s made money.

The main force driving the rise in stock prices in the 1980s was not improved profitability. It was the massive shift of investors' dollars into the stock market because of falling inflation. As we pointed out in chapter 2, high inflation during the 1970s had artificially raised the returns on hard assets, such as real estate, commodities, and collectibles, compared with the returns on stocks, bonds, and money market investments. As a result, investors shifted nearly one-tenth of their total assets—nearly $2 trillion—from securities into hard assets during the second half of the 1970s. This shift depressed bond values and pushed interest rates up, and wiped out nearly half the real value of the stock market. That's why the Dow had fallen to less than 800 by early 1982.

The fact that investors' portfolios were so heavily skewed toward hard assets at the beginning of the 1980s acted like a drawn bowstring once inflation began turning the corner. When oil prices cracked and inflation began falling in 1981, investors climbed over each other's backs in their attempts to unload their bloated hard assets in order to buy stocks and bonds. But with inflation headed south there were, not surprisingly, few ready and willing buyers, and the bottom fell out of hard-asset prices, leading to actual deflation in the mid-1980s. Meanwhile, everyone scrambled to buy securities, stock and bond prices soared, and interest rates tumbled. This tremendous decline in the cost of capital for American investors pushed stock prices higher—a rising tide that lifted all boats.

Most of the gains in the stock market from the time the bull market left the starting gate in August 1982, through the end of 1986, were caused by rising *valuations*, not by improved company performance. Stock prices rose, even though profits and book values remained flat, because the decline in interest rates made investors willing to pay more per dollar of earnings, cash flow, or book value. Many investors were even smart enough to look behind the reported earnings numbers and see that companies were getting stronger, selling excess assets, writing off inflated book values, and paring their overhead expenses.

So the allocation of assets, not security selection, was the key to successful portfolio management in the 1980s. The key decision was *whether* you were invested in stocks, bonds, money market investments, or real assets, not which securities within each asset class you owned. One of the unfortunate side effects of this "no-brainer" investment climate was that a lot of investors, especially the young ones who had entered the market after August 1982, began to believe that you always made money in the stock market. In many quarters, old-style, hard-nosed security analysis, associated with names such as Ben Graham and Warren Buffett, went out of style. Fortunately, the November 1987 blow-off in stock prices demolished the myth that making money in the stock market requires no work and restored a much-needed measure of discipline.

Companies, Not Sectors

The 1990s, however, will be the decade of the security analyst, not the asset allocator. The real profits will be earned through old-fashioned green eyeshade company analysis. From now on, investors are going to have to do their homework to pick successful investments. The portfolio shift that set up the big asset price changes in the 1980s is now finished. This means that investors can no longer count on falling interest rates and rising valuations to fuel rising stock prices the way they could in the mid-1980s. Further gains in stock prices will have to be earned the old-fashioned way—by improving the profitability of the individual companies that make up the market.

Successful stock market investors must recognize this change in the character of the market and shift the focus of their research efforts away from studying macroeconomic trends and toward identifying companies whose managers are doing an exceptional job managing their capital resources, away from asset allocation, and toward thoughtful security selection. This means identifying companies with management teams who are actively taking the steps described in chapter 7 to deploy their capital resources effectively. A portfolio of stocks selected on the basis of management quality and broadly diversified across industries is *the* strategy for the 1990s.

Of course, some companies will have both good managers and good markets at the same time. As always, there will be some sectors of the economy where it will be easier to earn profits than others. The 1990s, for example, will likely be kinder to capital goods producers than it will to financial service firms. Capital goods producers already endured their tough times in the early 1980s when U.S. manufacturers slashed their capital spending budgets in order to restructure for low inflation. Those who survived are leaner, tougher, and better managed as a result. Costs are down, productivity is up, and balance sheets are so clean they squeak—they are living examples of the principles of blue flame management discussed in chapter 7. Now that the world is growing again, and manufacturers in the United States and abroad are retooling and adding capacity, capital goods producers are enjoying sharp increases in the demand for their products. With both good managers and strong markets, they should do well in the 1990s.

In contrast, financial service companies will have tougher sledding in the decade ahead. In the 1980s, Wall Street firms rode the wave of expanding financial markets and falling interest rates to record profits. Now they find themselves with bloated payrolls and poor financial controls. Banks and savings-and-loan profits will be dragged down by the massive costs of cleaning up their real estate, farm, and foreign loan portfolios, and with rebuilding the deposit insurance funds that were depleted during the 1980s. Strong economic growth around the world means that further substantial reductions in interest rates are unlikely. And financial service firms are not well situated to profit from the predominant themes of the U.S. economy in the 1990s: capital expansion and rising exports.

The Business Cycle Is Changing

There is a third factor, in addition to disinflation and tax reform, that has had an important effect on both the economy and the way stocks are priced.

Financial deregulation, by severing the link between interest rates and recessions, may have permanently altered the cyclical behavior of the U.S. economy. That doesn't mean that we will never see a recession again. But it does mean they will be different, less frequent, less severe, and less pervasive than we have seen in the past. And it means that corporate cash flows will be more stable, an event that is going to have important implications for both corporate finance and stock prices in the 1990s.

According to the textbook timetables, a recession is supposed to show up once every four years, whether you need it or not. Since we are now in our seventh year of uninterrupted growth, many economists are standing on the platform, pulling out their watches, and staring down the track, expecting the next recession to show up any minute.

Changes in the structure of the economy in the 1980s mean that we are going to have to throw our old timetable away. In the good old days—back when the recession timetables made sense—booms and busts were virtually the exclusive province of the Federal Reserve. Study after study done during the 1960s and 1970s provided overwhelming evidence that sudden changes in the growth rate of the money supply dominated all other factors in explaining the major swings in output and employment. Moreover, these studies showed invariably that when the Fed pulled back on the reins of credit, six to nine months later we would have a recession.

The Fed's medicine was potent in those days because it had the ability to shut down the credit markets with a wave of its wand. A piece of legislation called Regulation Q set the maximum interest rate that banks were allowed to pay on their customers' deposits. This was a great deal for bankers, a sort of profit-margin insurance, because it acted to hold down their biggest cost of business. But it also made the economy prone to frequent recessions. Here's how it worked: If the Federal Reserve grew worried that the economy was beginning to overheat, all it had to do was pull back on the reins of credit by slowing the growth of bank reserves. This in turn pushed up interest rates on the open market. As soon as the rates had increased by enough to bump up against the ceilings set by Regulation Q—which in those days were only 5 percent—depositors figured out that they could get a lot better deal on (uncontrolled) Treasury bills and money market funds than they could on bank accounts. So they pulled their money out of the banks, an event that became so common that it eventually acquired its own name— "disintermediation." Of course, with money flowing out instead of in, banks were forced to slam their loan windows shut, and consumers and businesses were quickly forced to curtail their buying plans. Without money to lubricate the wheels of commerce, they quickly ground to a halt and the economy slipped into recession.

Regulation Q was swept out the door as part of the financial deregulation exercise at the turn of the decade, in order to ensure the banking system had a more steady supply of funds. In that regard, it has been a total success. Cynics complain that it isn't much of an improvement— before, banks loaned money at reasonable rates but they didn't have any—now you can't afford it. At least today the banks always have money to lend—it is just a question of price.

Recessions back then were national events. When interest rates bumped up against the Regulation Q ceilings, banks *all over the country* felt the pinch on the same day. So we tended to have recessions in Texas at the same time as California and New York, and recessions in the steel industry tended to look a lot like recessions in autos, chemicals, and home building. When things were going badly, there was nowhere to hide. We all had recessions together, and we all recovered together. But those days are gone forever.

Without Regulation Q, the Federal Reserve no longer has the ability to stop the music by abruptly shutting off credit to the banking system all over the country. Today when the Fed tries to tighten credit, and interest rates rise, the decision to borrow is up to the customer and his banker, based on individual circumstances. Rising interest rates still squeeze out borrowers, but not all borrowers, in all industries, in all parts of the country on the same day.

By taking away the band leader's baton, financial deregulation has effectively decoupled the parts of the economy, like the boxcars on a train. Now booms and busts are more regional affairs. Since 1982, for example, there has been a depression going on in the United States every day. First it was the manufacturers, then the oil patch, then the farmers, then real estate. It just keeps moving around! And there has been a boom going on somewhere, too. But when you average all the regions, all the sectors, and all the industries together, what you see is seven years of steady growth of 2 to 3 percent per year.

Because of this decoupling, the numbers for the whole economy don't mean what they used to mean, and historical comparisons don't make a lot of sense. In fact, it wouldn't be too far wrong to say that we don't have an "economy" anymore at all—we have a kind of common market where we all use the same money and speak (more or less) the same language, but each region of the country has its own pattern of economic activity. To stretch the point, with enough regional variation, it would be possible for every state in the union to have a recession every four years, just like the old days, but for the national economy—which is simply the sum of all the states—to grow every year. That's not going to happen, of course. But recessions won't follow the historical patterns in the future either. They will be less frequent, less severe, with more regional variation than we have seen in the past. And without the Regulation Q trigger, spending and economic growth are growing to be less sensitive to interest rates. If the Federal Reserve set out in earnest to produce an abrupt slowdown in the economy today, it would take sky-high interest rates to do the job.

Cash Flows Are Becoming Steadier

This line of reasoning also helps to explain some of the changes we are seeing in corporate balance sheets. A company whose business is spread around the country will have much steadier cash flows than before, since it is less likely that all of their important markets will go in the tank at the same time. This means they are less likely to become insolvent, and can afford to be run with a little more debt and less equity than they have been in the past.

Many members of Congress have expressed alarm over the rise of corporate indebtedness that has occurred in the 1980s. The fact is, however, that more than 95 percent of the increased corporate debt that Congress is now so worried about has been concentrated in the food, utility, and nondurable manufacturing sectors—the sectors where cash flows are the most stable. Ironically, smoother cash flows also make healthy companies with high returns and little debt extremely attractive as take-over candidates.[*]

The stock market is becoming more aware of this fact by pushing up the values of steady cash producers relative to the general market (such as the tobacco and food companies). In the 1990s, stock market investors will increasingly shift their focus from asset values to cash flows as they learn that with less frequent, less severe recessions, manufacturing companies can have steady cash flows, too.

Epilogue

"That was a fine term paper that you turned in on 'America's Second Industrial Revolution,' Rick," said Profes-

---

[*] A company with a 20 percent return on equity and no debt, for example, would have a 60 percent return if its cash flows are steady enough to run at four parts debt to one part equity.

sor Marshall. "You showed a real understanding of the forces that turned our economy inside out and got us back on the growth track again fifty years ago back in the 1990s. Based on your paper, I'd say you spent most of your spring break sitting in front of the laserfilm reading machine in the business library. You can be very proud of your effort."

"Thanks, Professor Marshall. I guess I did put in a little overtime on the paper. But the more I read, the more I wanted to understand what really happened back then. And besides, reading laserfilms beats blowing the dust off the covers of fifty-year-old copies of *Business Week.* I was fascinated with the way the country got hooked on inflation and tax shelters in the 1970s, and people were pushed into building all those hotels and shopping centers while we let our factories wear out and fall apart. The disinflation and tax reform, which they called Reaganomics in the 1980s and which threw the country into a cold-turkey withdrawal from the excesses of the 1970s, was especially interesting. I think that's what exposed the damage that had been done to the stock of industrial capital and forced people to rebuild their companies. And I'm convinced that's what set up the phenomenal capital expansion that fueled the growth boom of the 1990s.

"But one thing really puzzles me. Looking back on the 1990s, it seems so obvious that the foundations had already been laid for a phenomenal industrial expansion by 1990. Falling inflation and tax reform had restored people's incentives to work and had redirected the stream of savings dollars away from hotels and shopping centers and back toward building factories. The capital shortage and high real returns had produced a shareholder revolt that jolted the managers of public companies out of their lethargy, and forced them to rebuild their companies from the ground up. We had been on the receiving end of a giant reverse Marshall Plan—more than $500 billion of foreign capital, in the form of new machines and new factories, had been brought into the United States through the trade accounts in the

1980s. And the Baby Boom generation was just leaving the BMW-Reebok-Perrier years and entering middle age, getting ready to unleash a tidal wave of savings into the financial markets during the 1990s.

"You've always taught us in class that there are only two things that really matter for economic growth, Professor Marshall. Whether people want to work, and whether they have the tools they need to do their jobs. And obviously, both were in place before the 1990s arrived. Then shouldn't it have been obvious that the United States would take off on a real growth binge in the 1990s?"

"It certainly should have, Rick."

"But judging from the articles written at the time, the economists spent the whole time wringing their hands over the federal government's budget deficit and the trade deficit. And the politicians were preoccupied with looking for excuses to raise tax rates and trying to devise plans to bash foreign investors. The second American industrial revolution was right there in front of their faces the whole time. Why didn't anyone see it coming?"

"Well, Rick, have you ever heard about 'the curious incident of the dog in the nighttime'? "

Index